BY MASAHIRO CHATANI

ONDORI POP-UP ORIGAMIC ARCHITECTURE

★ Published by ONDORISHA PUBLISHERS, LTD., 11-11 Nishigoken-cho, Shinjuku-ku, Tokyo 162
★ Sole Overseas Distributor: Japan Publications Trading Co., Ltd.
P. O. Box 5030 Tokyo International, Tokyo, Japan.
★ Distributed in the United States by Kodansha America Inc.
114 Fifth Avenue, New York, NY 10011, U.S.A.
in British Isles & European Continent by Premier Book Marketing Ltd.,
1 Gower Street, London WC1E 6HA
in Australia by Bookwise International
54 Crittenden Road, Findon, South Australia 5023, Australia.

10 9 8

ISBN 0-87040-656-6
Printed in Japan

CONTENTS

Message from the Author

After trying for some time to design original greeting cards, I finally designed some unique pop-up cards by folding and cutting paper. These cards were so popular among my friends and now I would like to introduce them to you in this lovely book. When you open one of these folded post-card sized constructions, there is wondrous movement and a structure arises which is so interesting and fascinating that it captures your attention. The dreamy scene created by light and shadow invites you to a fantasy world.

Please try to make these unique cards by yourself by reproducing and developing shapes and spaces within folded paper twice as big as a post card. There are limitless possibilities in this art. Should you fail, do not give up. Remember that failure is the best teacher.

There are three kinds of construction in this book. Two of them are made with a single sheet of paper. Of these two forms, one is not meant to be opened at all and the other is to be opened to an angle of 90 degrees. These two forms are fairly simple and easy to make. Cards which are to be opened to an angle of 180 degrees are a little more difficult but they are well worth trying. To make this kind of card, cut and assemble the parts into the required form, and attach it onto the foundation paper with thread. When these cards are opened, a three-dimensional form emerges before your eyes. The unfolding process is unexpected and even if you try to draw a diagram or think about it, you may find it difficult to understand the mechanism. Some cards do not need to be unfolded. They look three-dimensional without opening. Imagination helps achieve this effect.

I do hope that boys and girls will foster their creativity through making these cards and that they will become fine architects in the future. I am thinking of spending my leisure after retirement making and playing with these cards.

Masahiro Chatani

Author: Masahiro Chatani

1967: Doctor of Engineering

1977: Visiting Associate Professor, University of Washington at Seattle

1980～: Professor, Tokyo Institute of Technology

Three-storied Pagoda

Instructions on page 27

Sacred Fire

Instructions on page 28

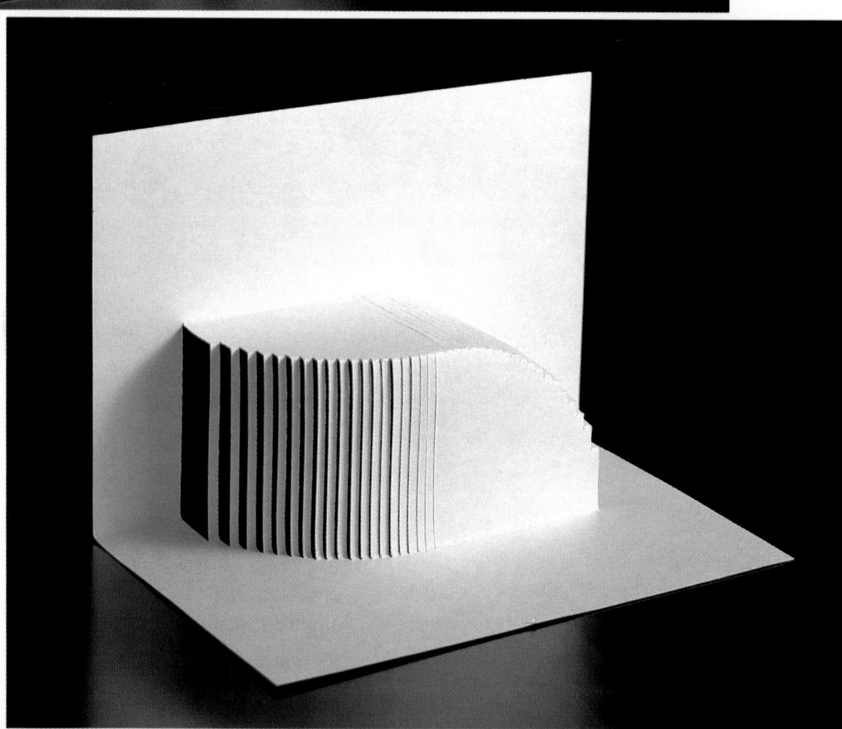

Block

Instructions on page 41

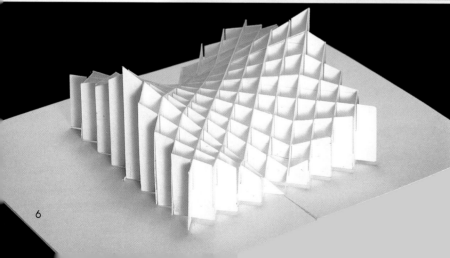

Sea Bottom Palace

Instructions on page 29

White Ghost

Instructions on page 31

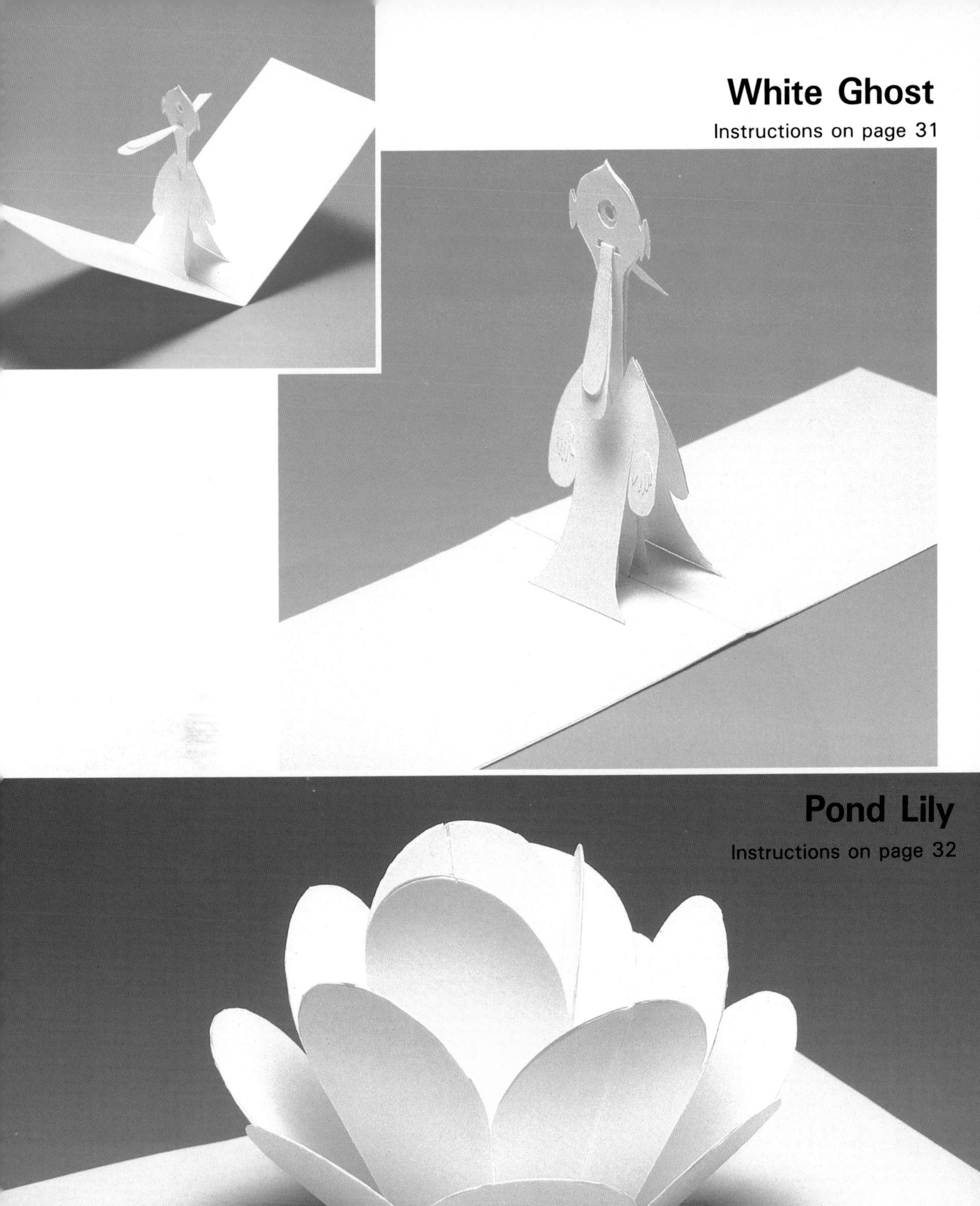

Pond Lily

Instructions on page 32

Japanese Dolls

Instructions on page 43

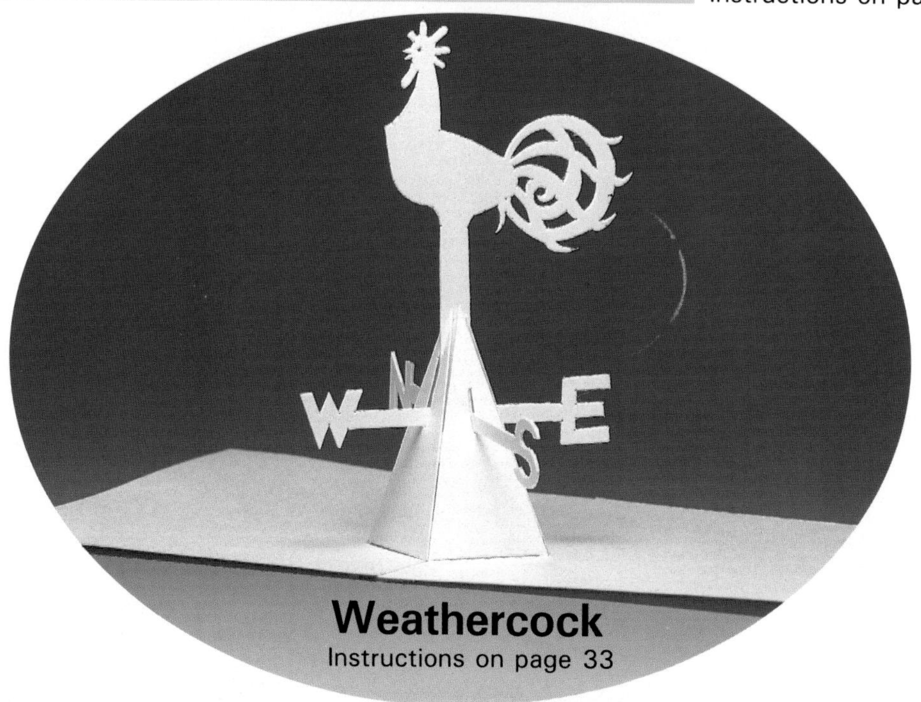

Weathercock

Instructions on page 33

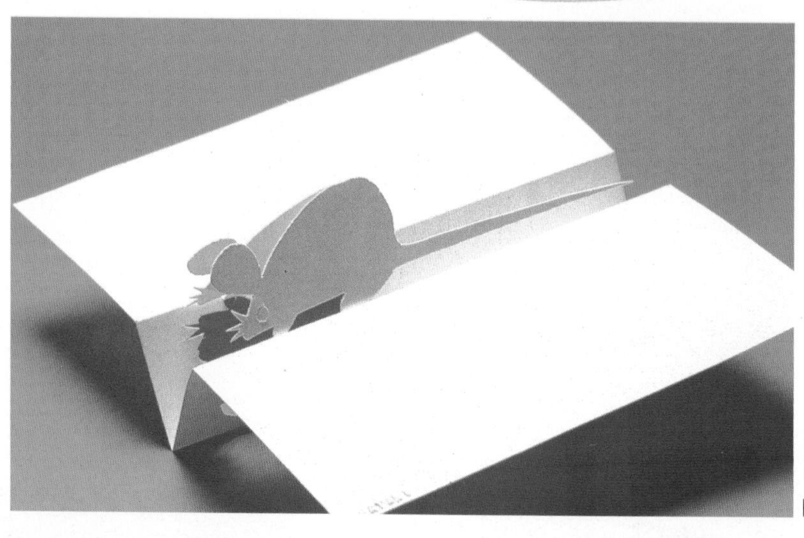

Mouse

Instructions on page 45

Diamond

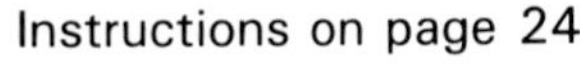

Instructions on page 24

Glass Gallery

Instructions on page 34

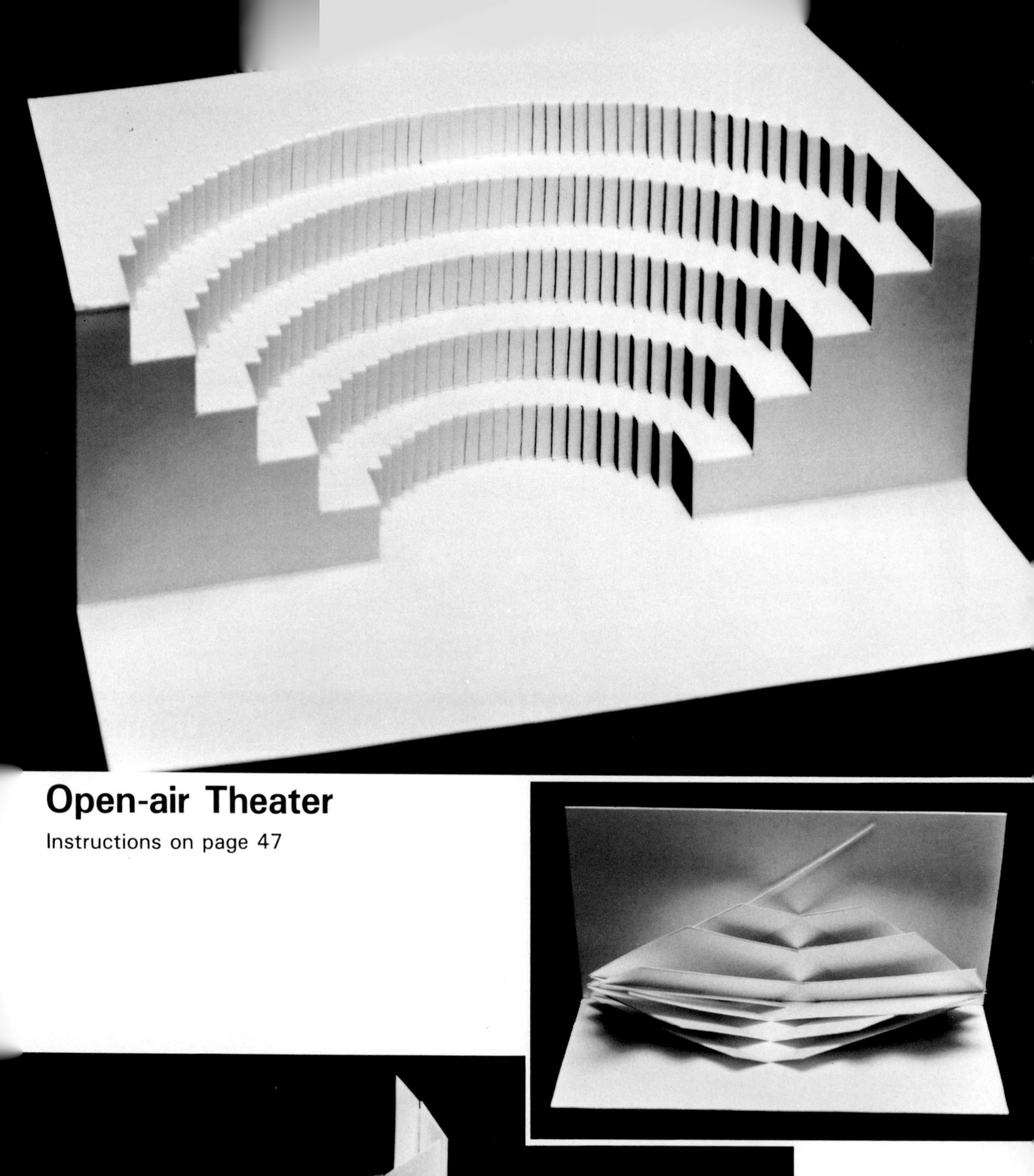

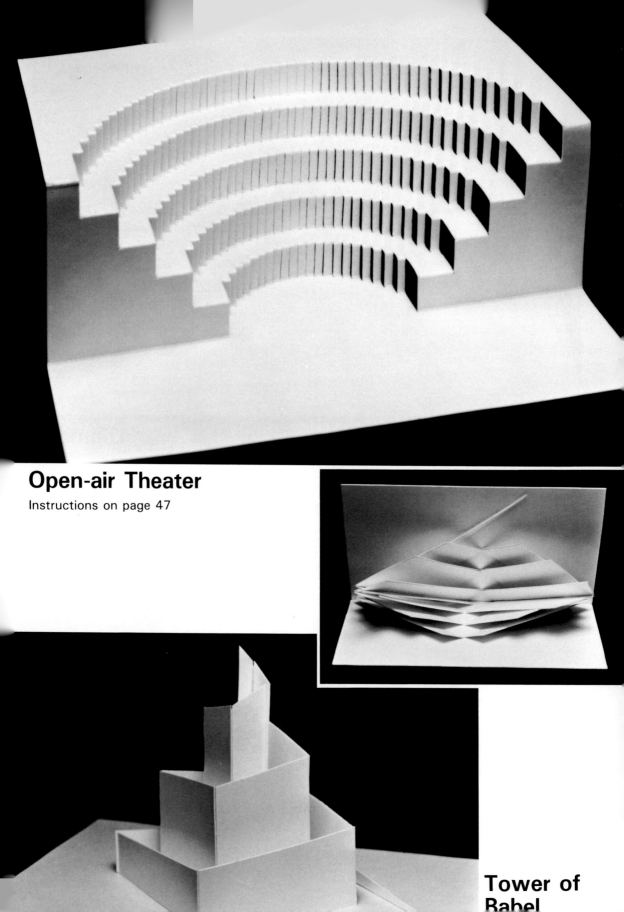

Open-air Theater

Instructions on page 47

Tower of Babel

White Chapel

Instructions on page 49

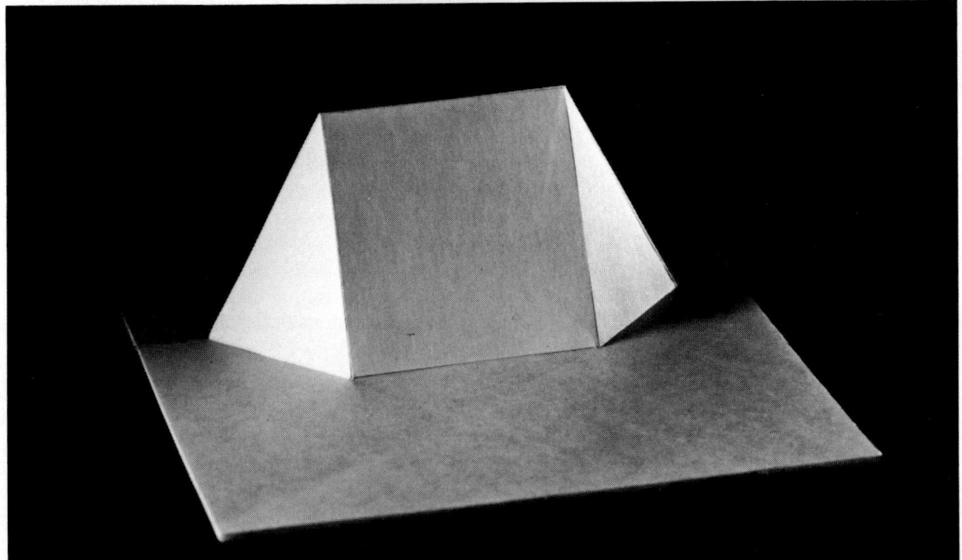

Tent

Instructions on page 22

Castle

Instructions on page 51

Funeral Temple

Instructions on page 30

Noh Stage

Instructions on page 36

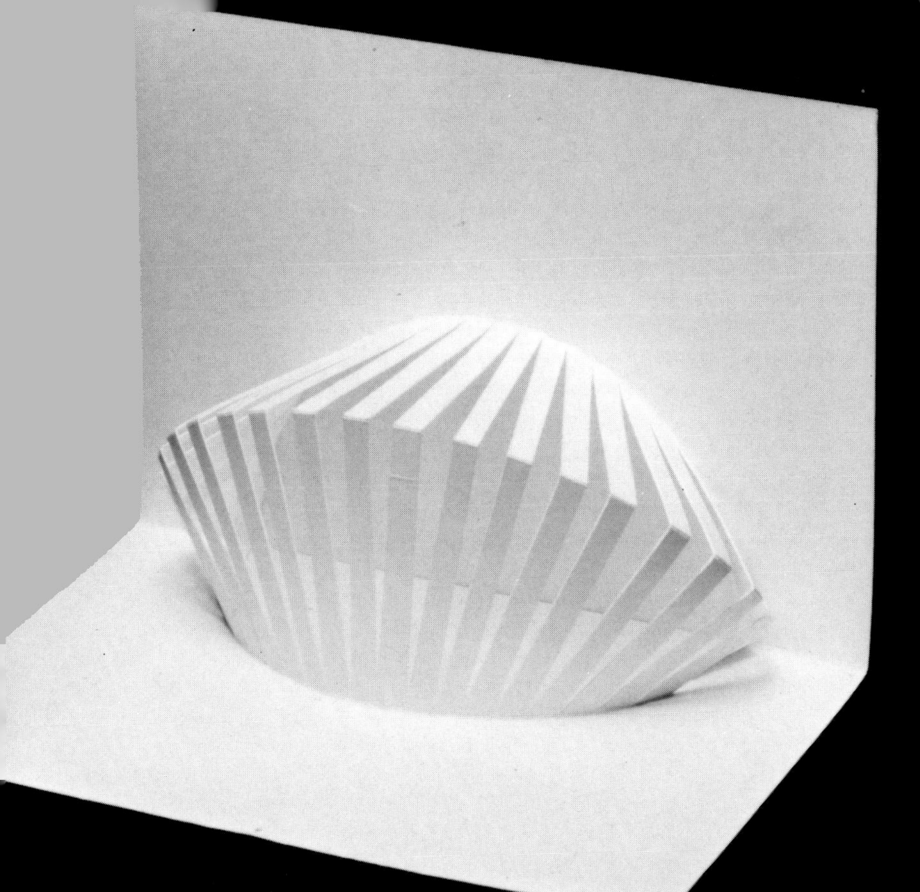

Music Shell

Instructions on page 53

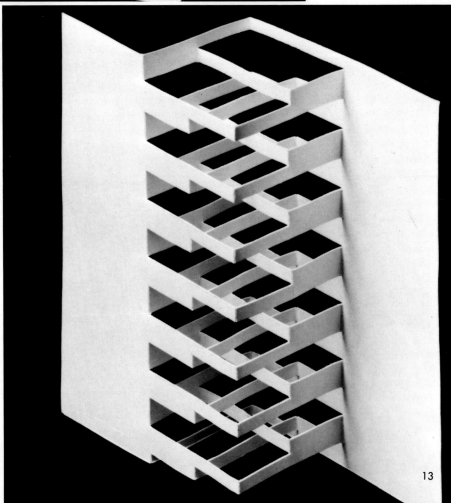

Grade Separation

Instructions on page 55

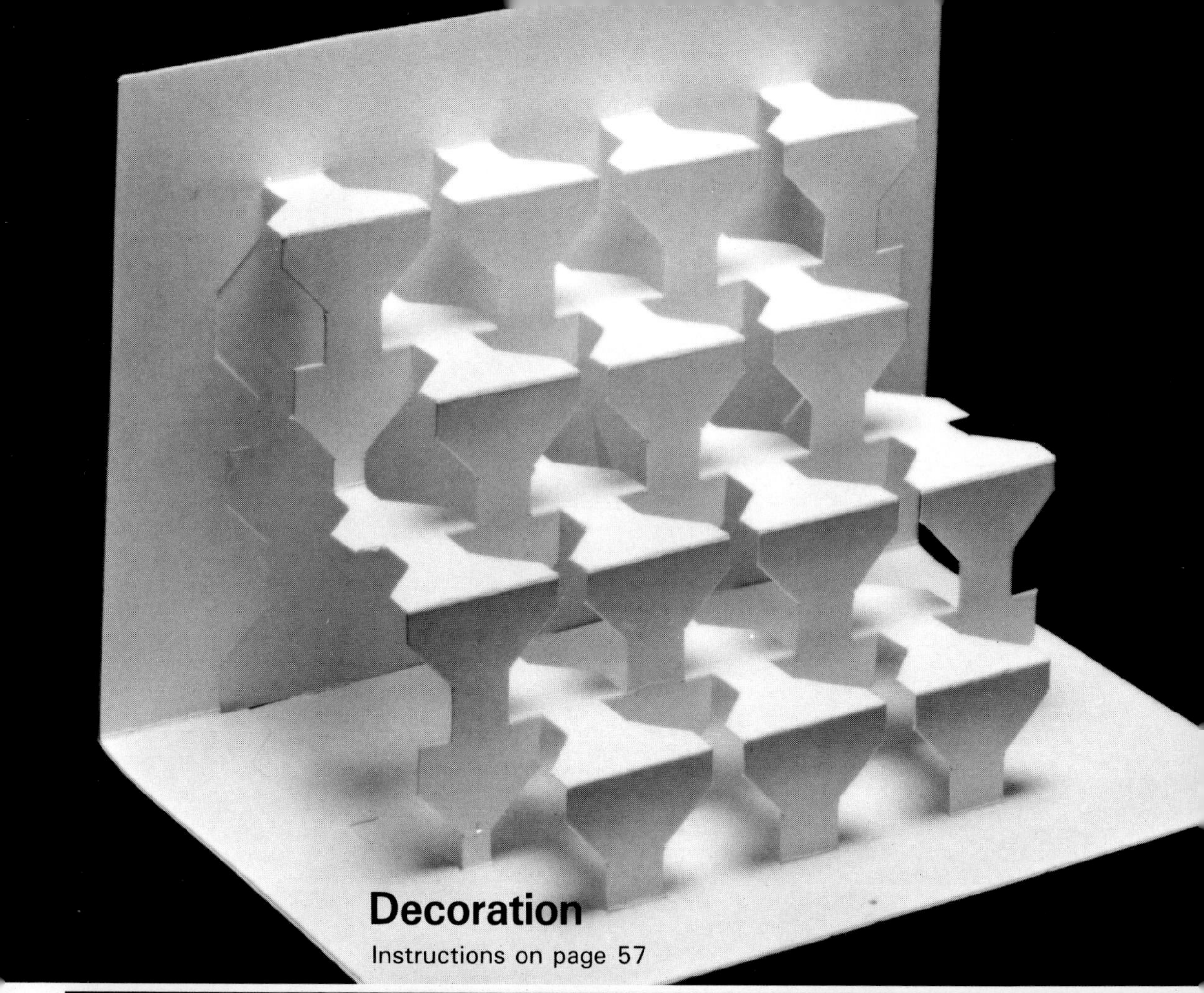

Decoration

Instructions on page 57

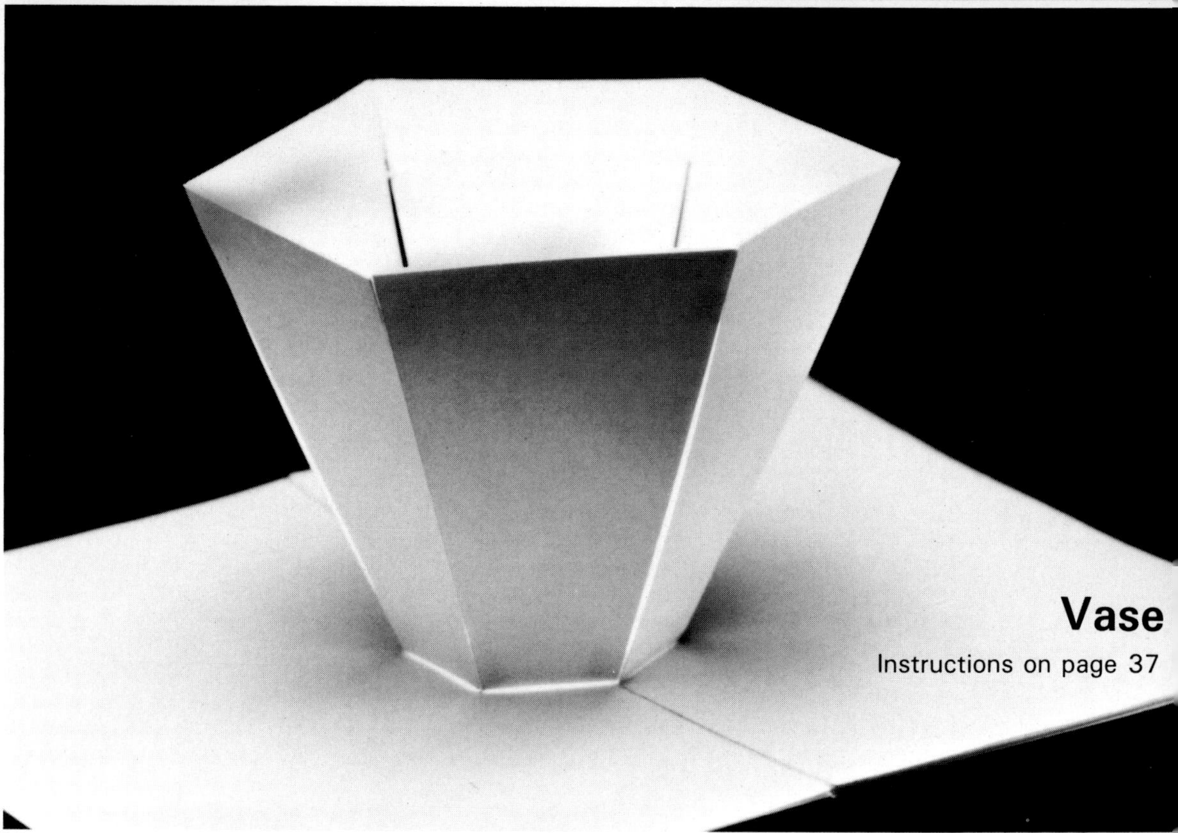

Vase

Instructions on page 37

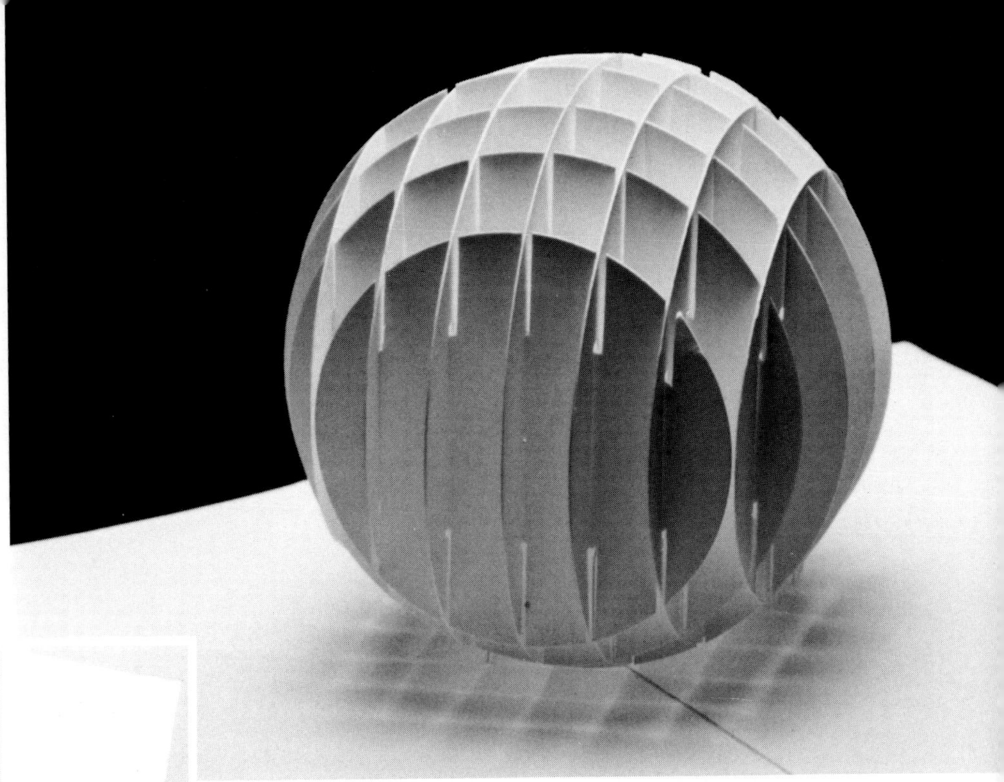

Globe

Instructions on page 38

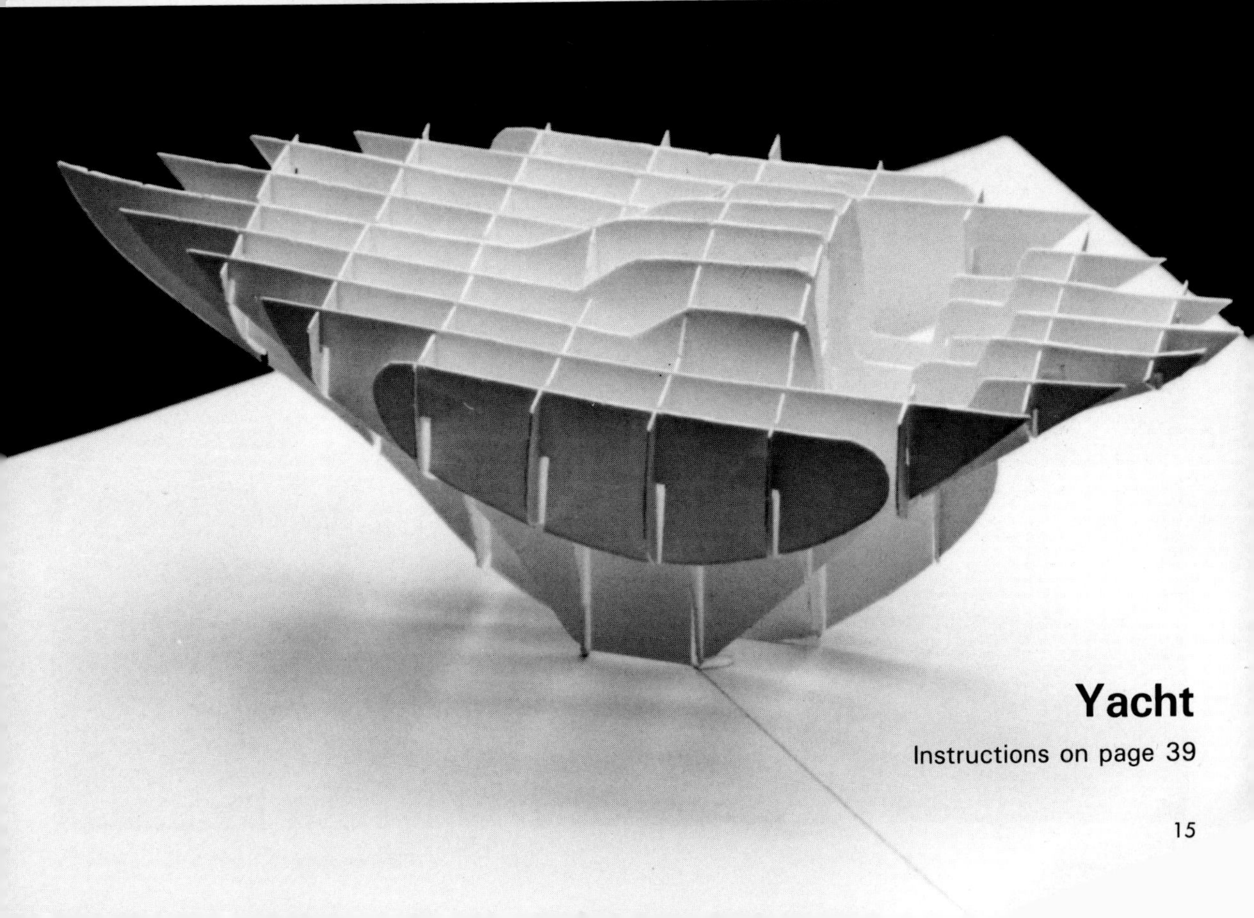

Yacht

Instructions on page 39

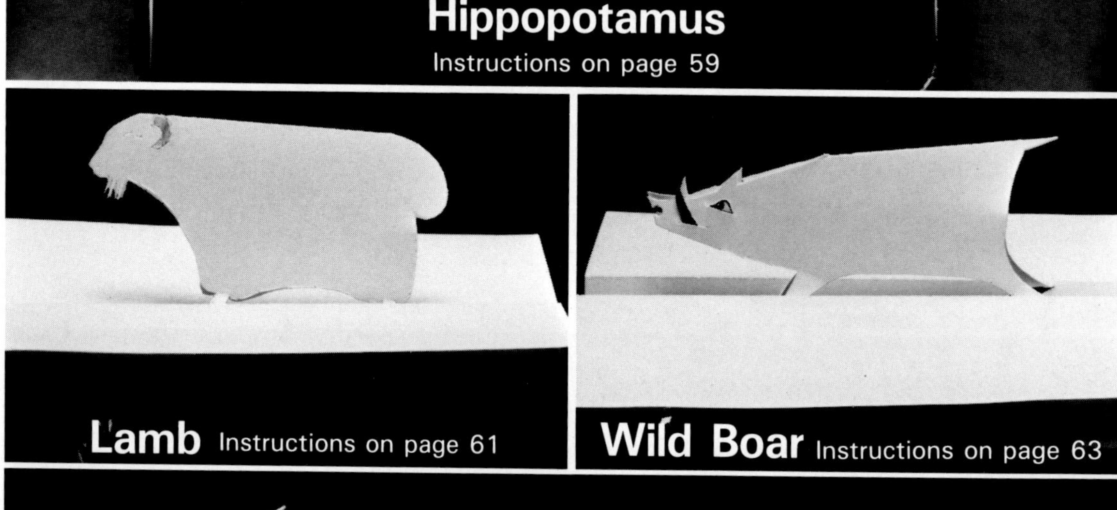

Hippopotamus
Instructions on page 59

Lamb Instructions on page 61

Wild Boar Instructions on page 63

Horse
Instructions on page 65

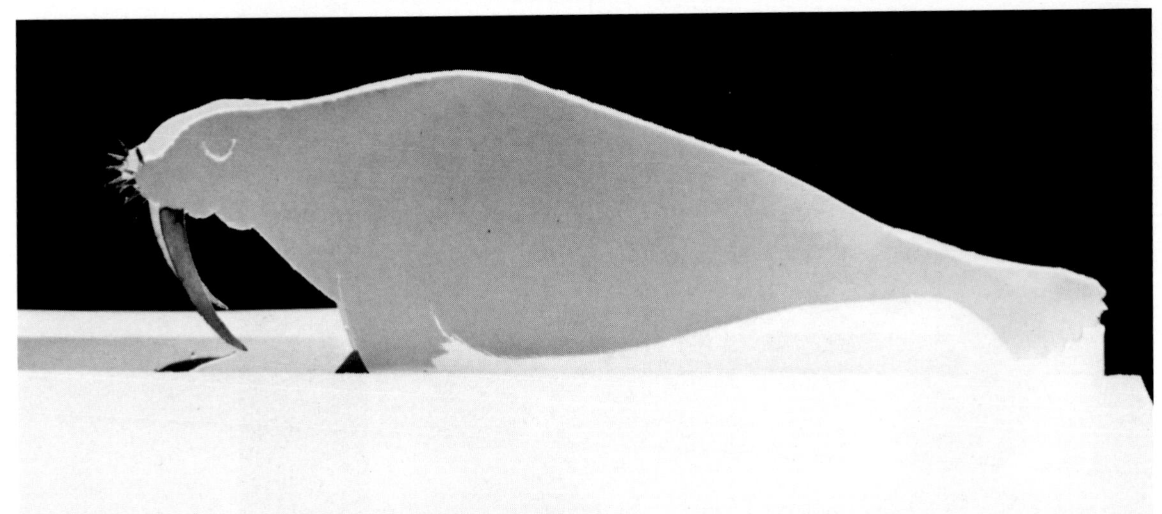

Walrus
Instructions on page 67

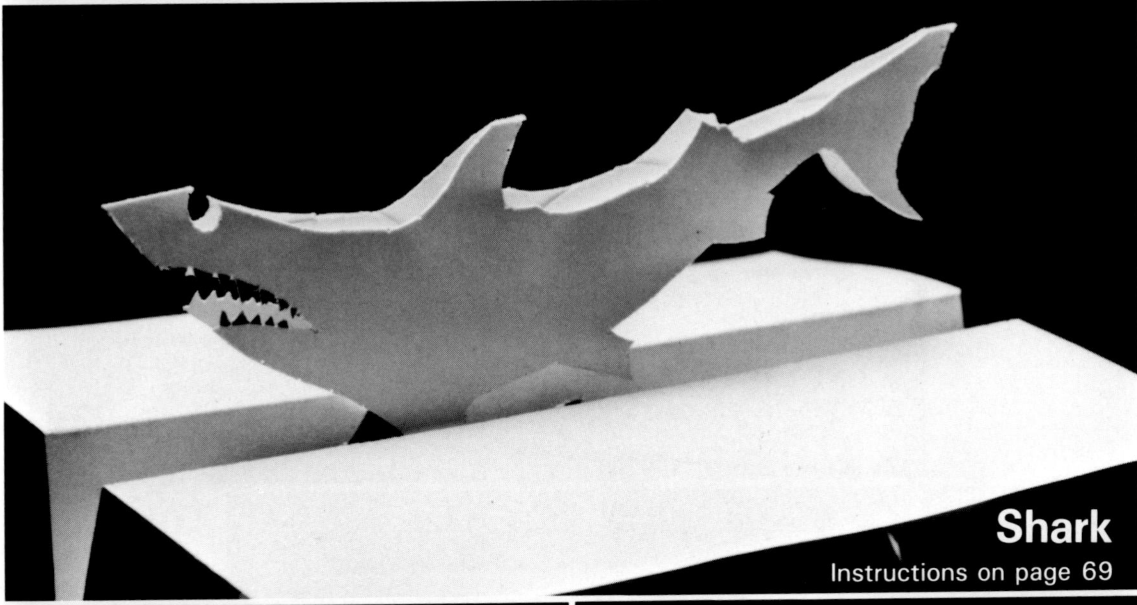

Shark
Instructions on page 69

Lion Instructions on page 71

Little Bear Instructions on page 73

Crab

Instructions
on page 75

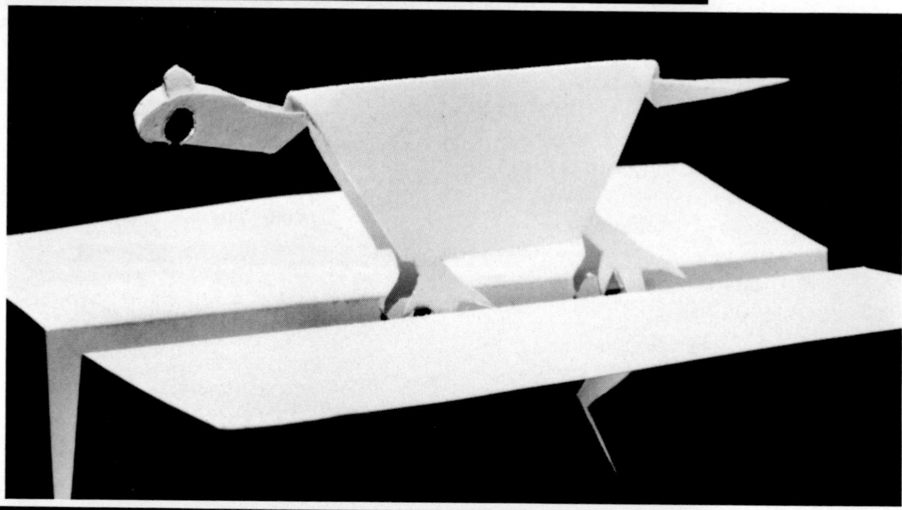

Tortoise

Instructions
on page 77

Mask

Instructions on
pages 79 and 81

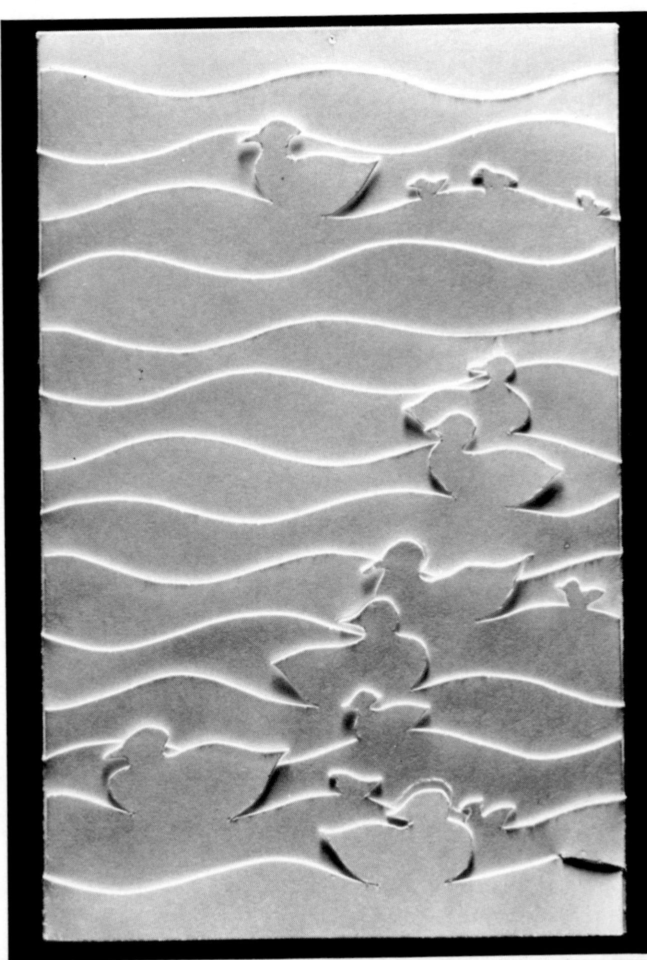

Waterbird
Instructions on page 83

Offshore Cruising
Instructions on page 85

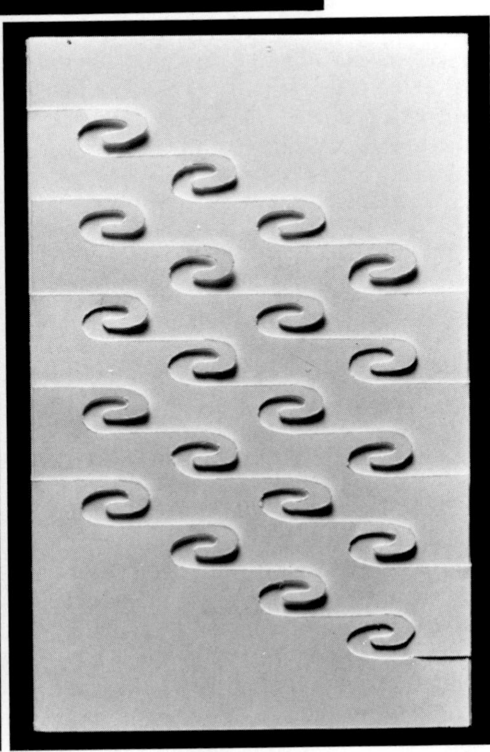

Stream
Instructions on page 87

● Basics in Origamic Architecture

Let's make the pop-up cards.

I. Materials and Tools

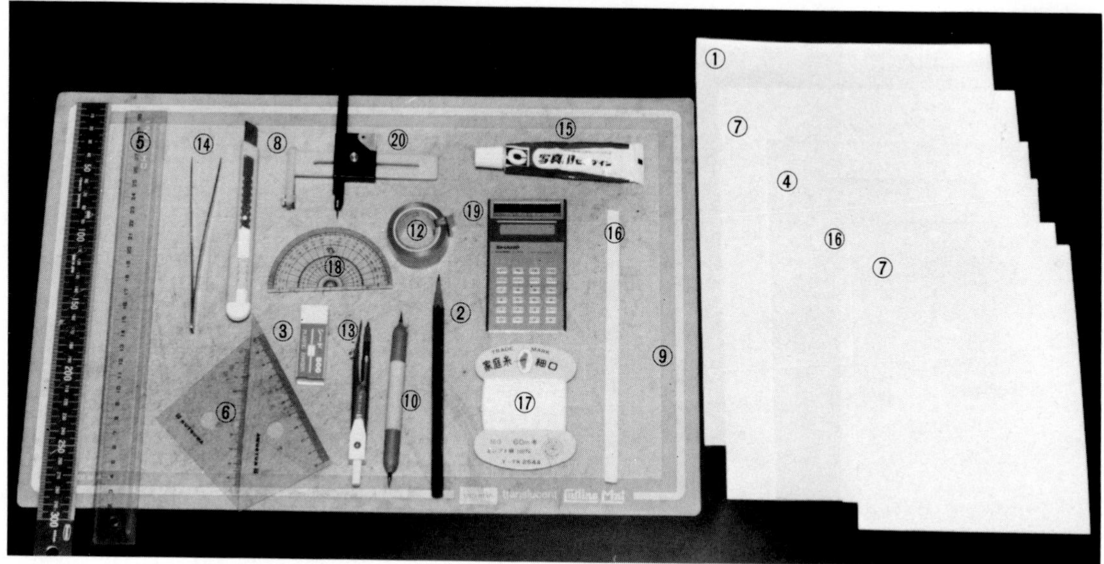

(1) Sketch pad (2) Pencil (3) Eraser (4) Graph paper (1mm square) (5) Scale (6) Set square (7) White Kent paper (8) Cutting knife (9) Cutting board (10) Thick and thin stylus pen (11) Steel ruler (12) Clear adhesive tape (13) Compasses (14) Pointed tweezers (15) All-purpose glue (16) Japanese rice paper (17) White cotton thread (18) Protractor (19) Calculator (20) Circle cutter (21) Small steel cutting plate.

The materials and tools required are different depending on what you are going to make. For the 90° open type, materials and tools numbered in the illustration 1 to 12 are required and in special cases those numbered 1 to 15. For the 180° and 360° open types, those numbered 1 to 17 and in special cases 1 to 20 are used. For the 0° type, tools numbered 1 to 12 are used. Buy the minimum number of tools at first and add one by one as necessary. Your head and hands are the most important tools. Let them work as much as possible.

II. Making the 0° type

Cut Kent paper into 15 cm by 30 cm. Fold one-third from each end. Unfold and place a pattern sheet over the base paper and dot along both folding and cutting lines with a thin stylus pen. (Another method is to trace the design with a pencil and transfer to the paper to be used. These pencil lines should be erased after the design is cut into the paper.) Unfold and cut along cutting lines. Overlap the cut pieces alternating left and right from the top. Make a slit at the end of the second wave from the last and insert the end of the last wave into the slit. (See page 83 for cutting and folding lines.)

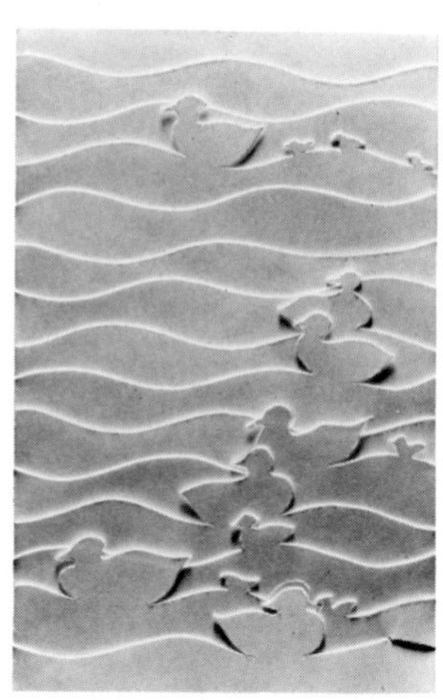

III. Making the 90° open type

The 90° patterns shown in this book can themselves be used as cards by removing from this book and cutting and folding as indicated. If using as a pattern book, cut Kent paper into 15 cm by 20 cm for the base. Then, trace the pattern onto graph paper, cover the base with the graph paper as shown in Fig. a, and dot along the cutting lines with a thin stylus pen (Fig. b). Cut along cutting lines (Fig. c), score fold lines with a stylus pen and fold. Another method of cutting is to place the pattern on the base and cut both the pattern and the base with a cutting knife. Fold the longest lines around the edges first using both hands and gradually complete the fold.

(a)

(b)

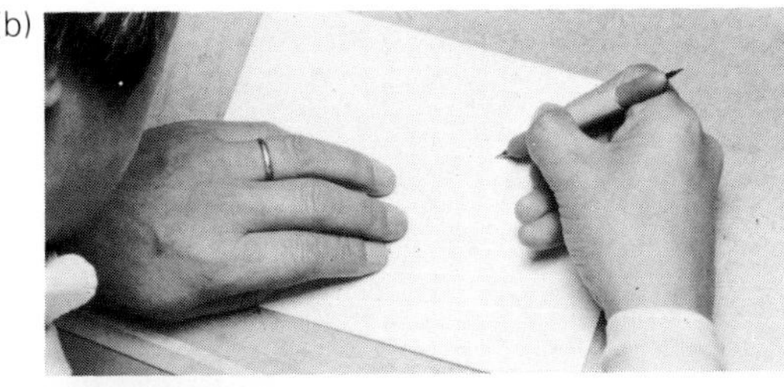

(c)

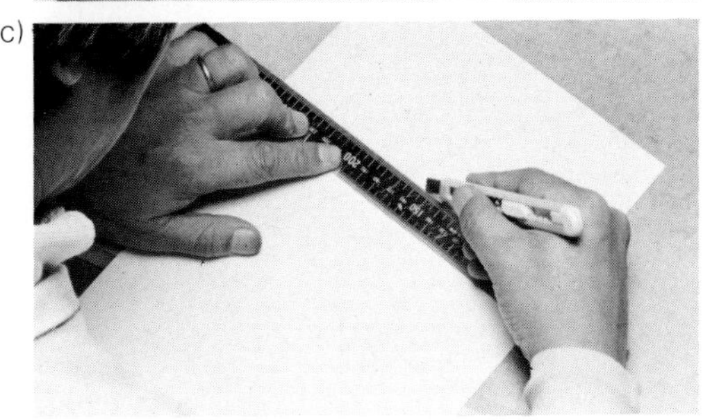

IV. Making the base for 180° open type

1. Cut 2 sheets of 15 cm by 10 cm for the base from Kent paper. Cut one strip of 15 cm by 1.5 cm from Japanese rice paper and apply all-purpose glue.
2. Place the base paper on this strip along the center line.
3. Place the second base paper on the remaining side of this strip.
4. Before the glue becomes completely dry, fold the paper from the joint. Japanese rice paper is easy to stretch when wet.

①

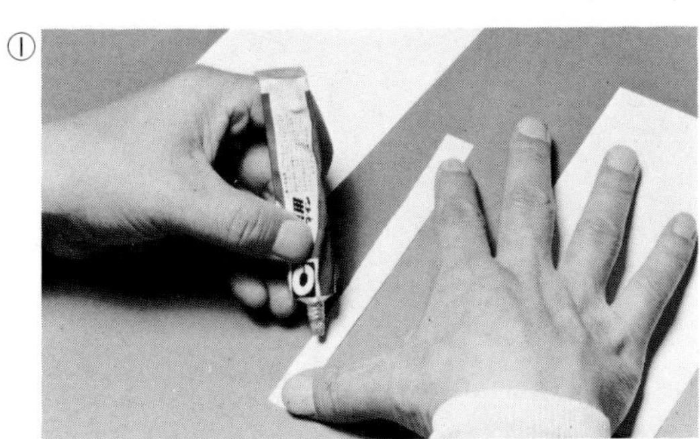

②

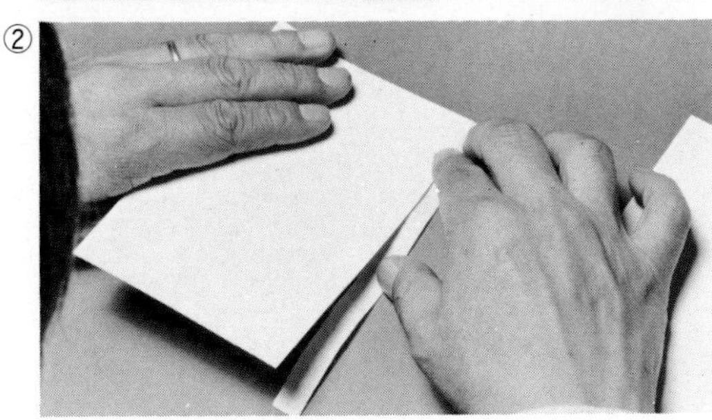

③

④

V. Step-by-step instructions for making the 180° open type

A: Tent

Shown on page 11

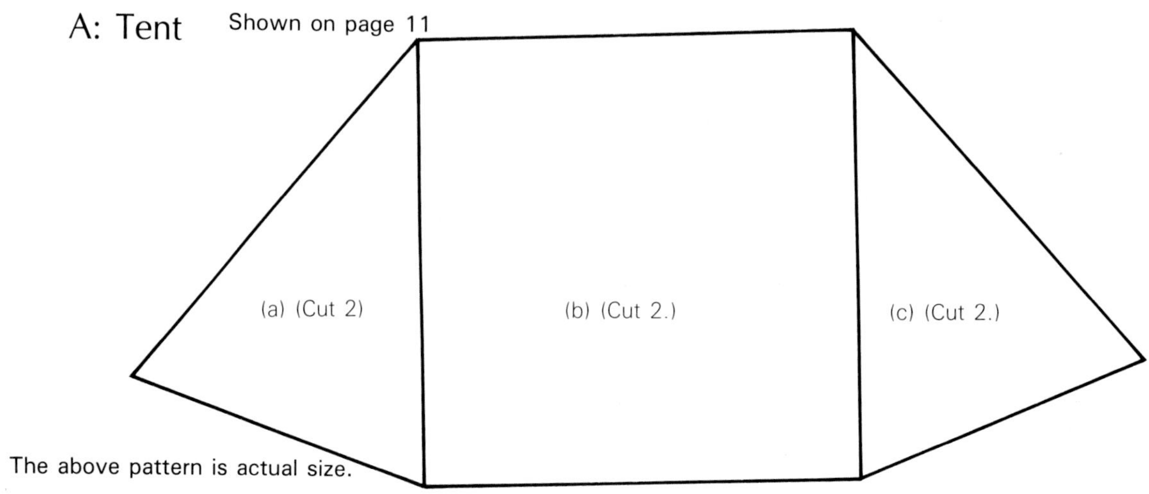

The above pattern is actual size.

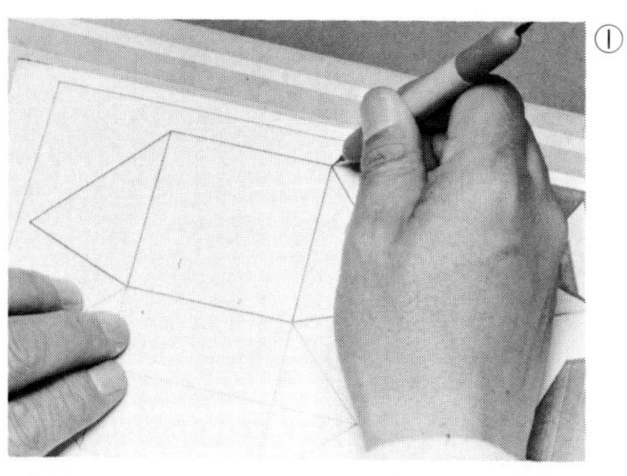
①

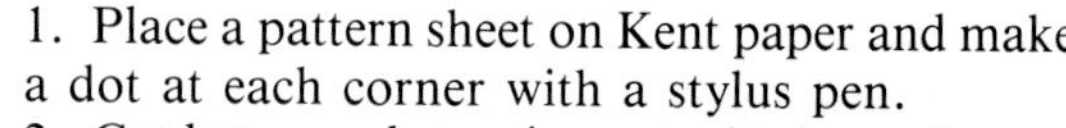

1. Place a pattern sheet on Kent paper and make a dot at each corner with a stylus pen.
2. Cut between dots using a steel ruler and a cutting knife.
3. Make sure that you cut all the required number of pieces.
4. Cut Japanese rice paper into small pieces and apply all-purpose glue using a pair of tweezers.
5. The photo shows how to join pieces of the tent.

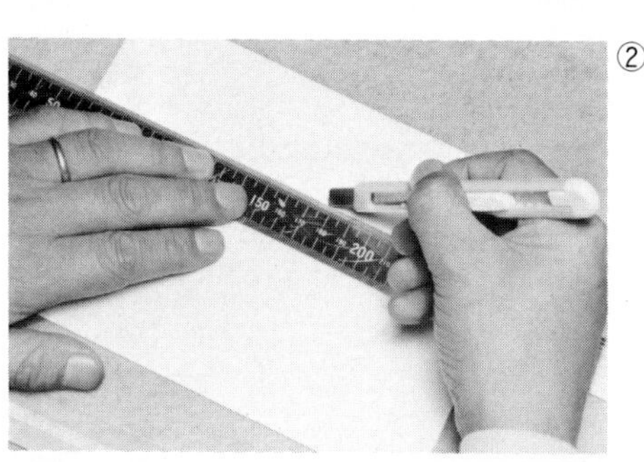
②

③

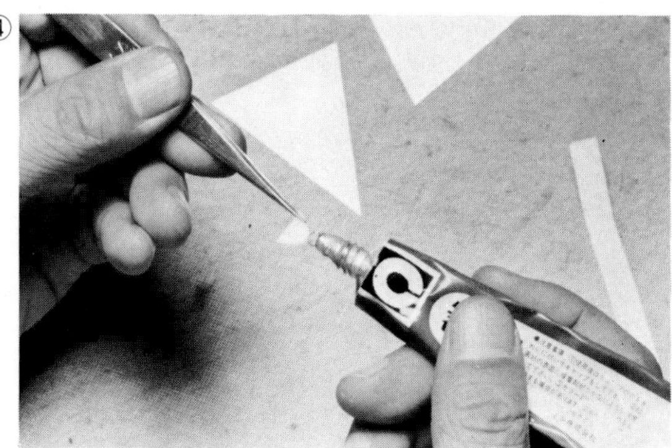
④

⑤

6. Before joining all pieces, glue cotton thread onto each corner.
7. Apply glue to Japanese rice paper and place on cotton thread to fix.
8. Join remaining pieces together.
9. The photo shows the assembled tent.
10. Place a pattern sheet on the base and make 4 holes with a stylus pen.
11. Insert the end of 4 pieces of thread into each of the holes and glue.

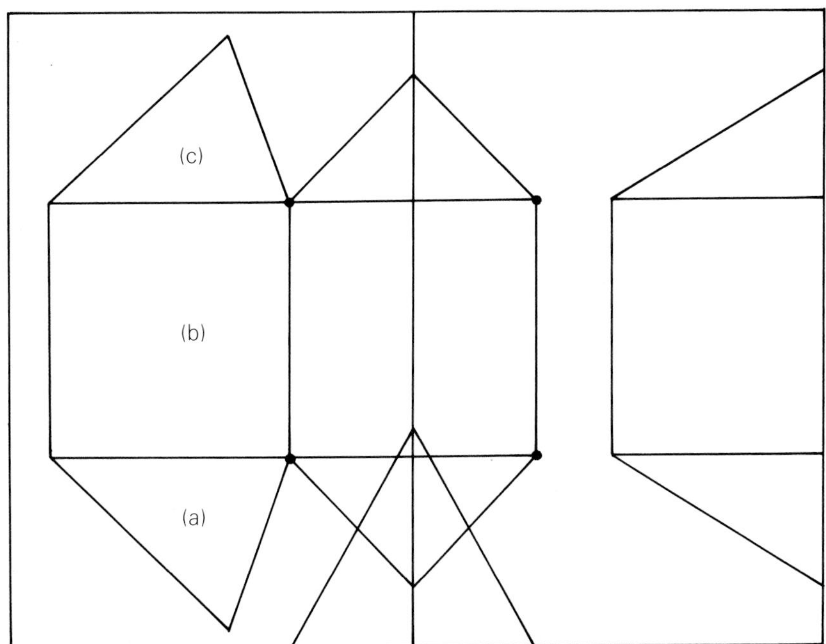

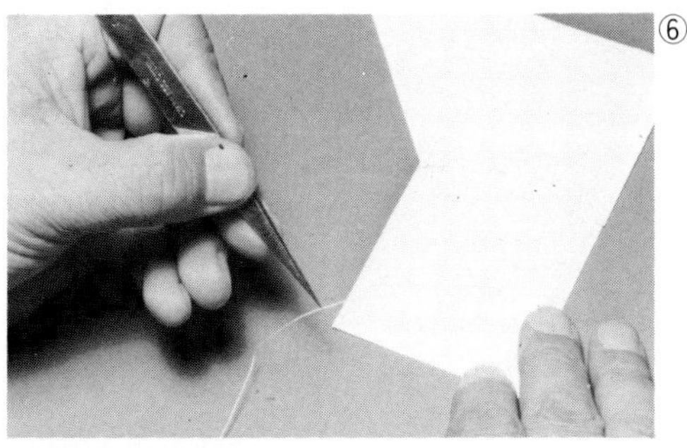
⑥

⑦

⑧

⑨

⑩

⑪

12. Pull the ends of thread from the opposite side of the base.
13. Fix the ends of thread temporarily with adhesive tape. Open the base and check the assembled tent.
14. Glue a small piece of Japanese rice paper onto the end of each thread.
15. Cut off excess thread and remove adhesive tape.
16. The photo shows the finished card.

⑫

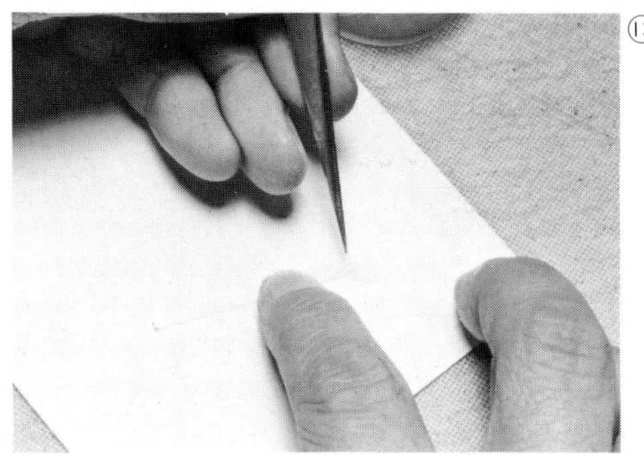
⑬

⑭

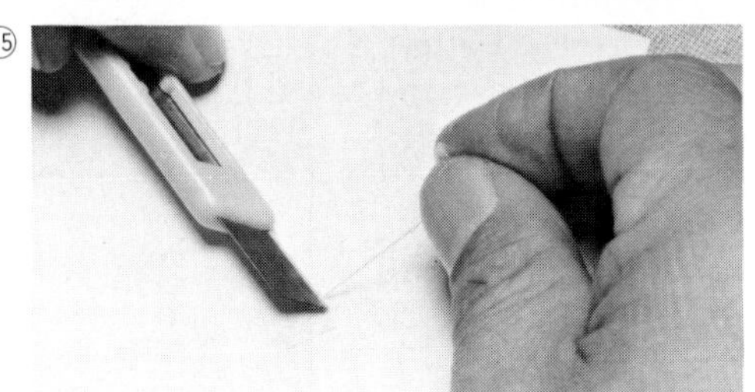
⑮

⑯

B: Diamond Shown on page 9

1. Cut out the required number of pieces using the patterns shown on the next page. Make sure that all the pieces are cut.
2. Start assembling using the bigger parts (a) and (b) for the center.
3. The photo shows how to join the part (c) with (a) and (b).
4. The photo shows how to join the part (f).
5. The finished diamond.

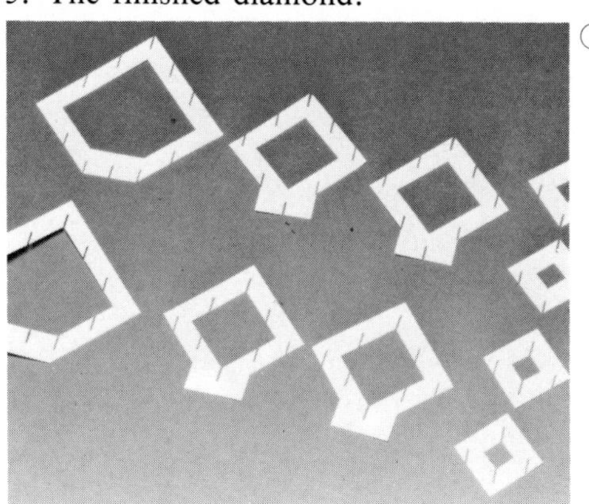
①

②

③

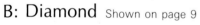

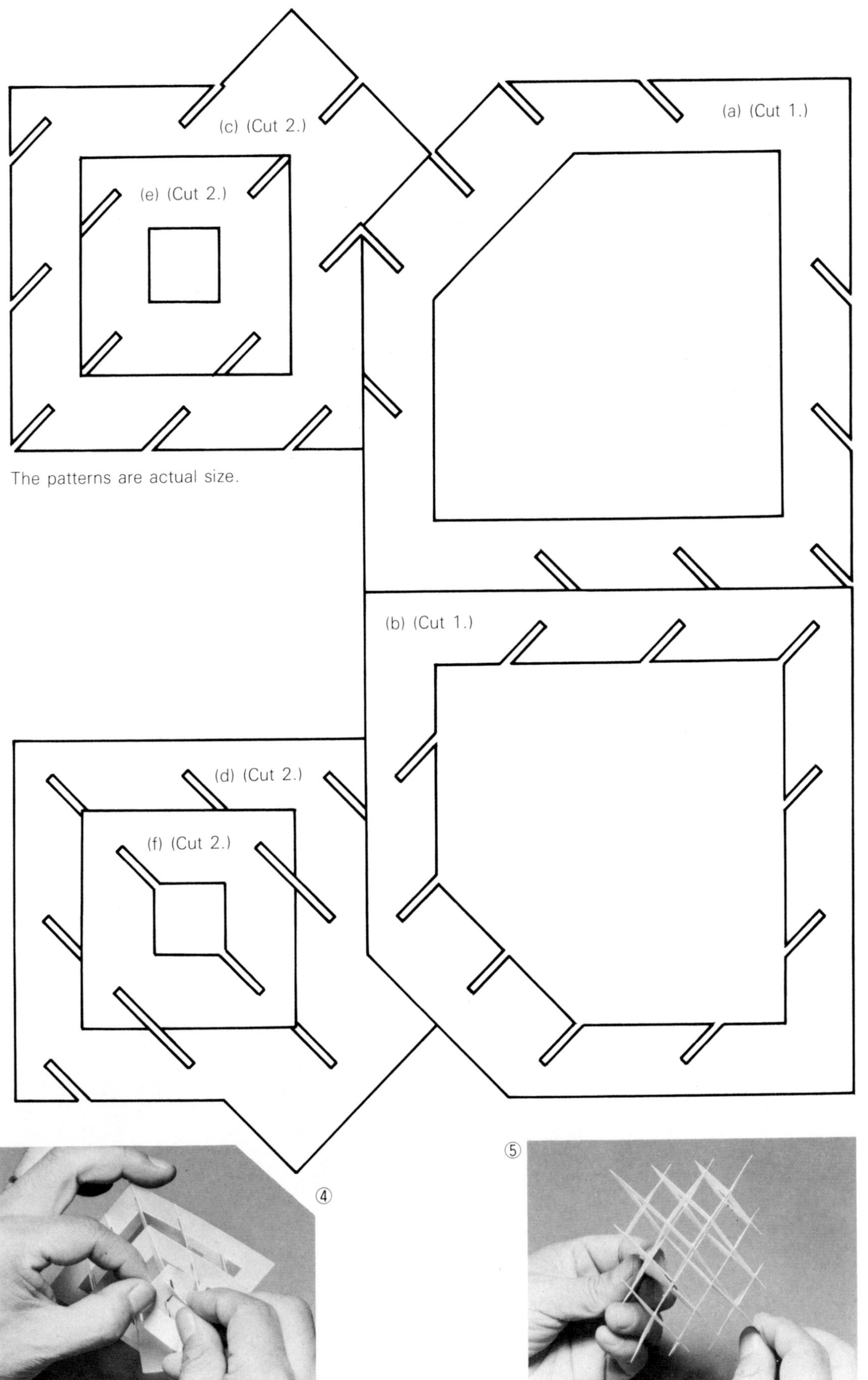

The patterns are actual size.

④

⑤

⑥

⑦

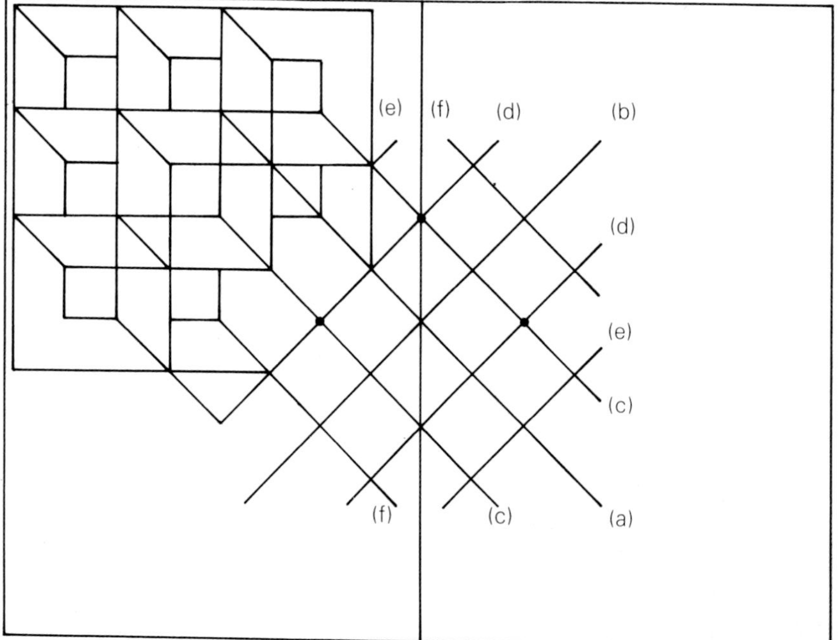

6. Check that all the pieces are joined together.
7. Attach thread at three places (shown with dots in the above diagram) and fix the finished diamond onto the base following the directions from 10 to 16 of "Tent."

Some of the 180° open types show the reverse side of the architecture and in this case, use very small pieces of Japanese rice paper for joining in order to hide the joints and the ends of thread.

After assembling all the pieces, join with the cube at the bottom with Japanese rice paper. Attach cotton thread at four corners of the finished torch and insert thread into the holes of the base (shown with dots).

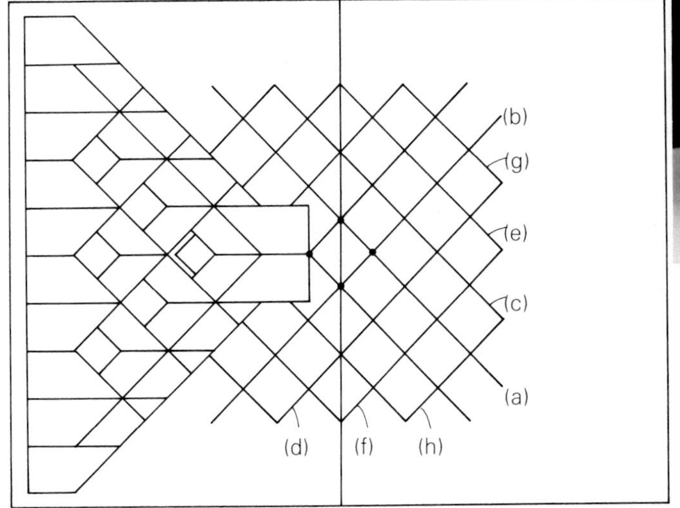

Sea Bottom Palace Shown on page 6

Cut out 30 pieces of 15 kinds of parts using the patterns below. Following the diagram on the next page, join them together starting with the biggest ones.
The patterns below are seven-tenths actual size.

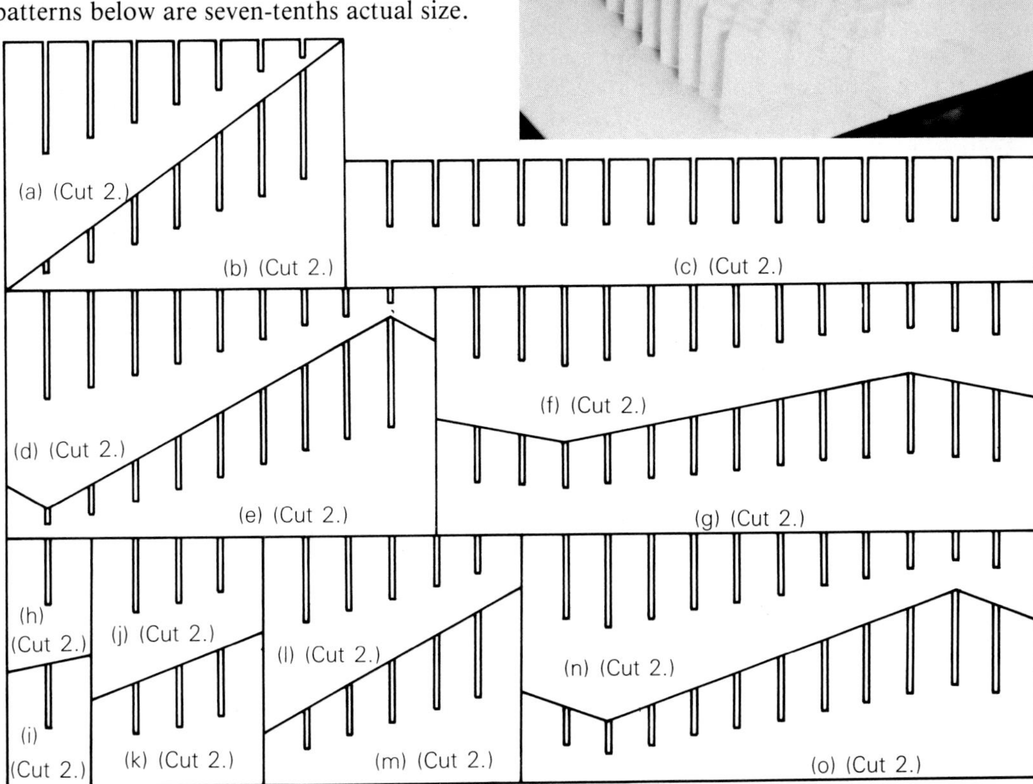

After assembling all the pieces, glue small pieces of Japanese rice paper onto each corner of the reverse side. Attach thread at the bottom of the longest pieces and insert the ends of thread into the holes of the base (shown with dots).

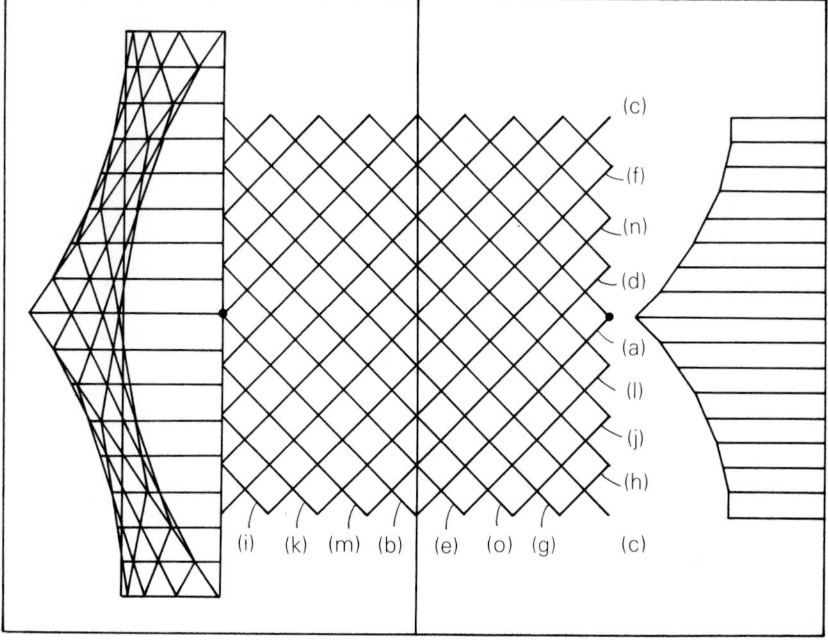

Funeral Temple Shown on page 12

Cut out 8 pieces each of (a) and (b) using the patterns below. Join all the pieces together with small pieces of Japanese rice paper glued to the reverse side of each component. Do not join the sides of (A). Attach the joined temple onto the base with thread.

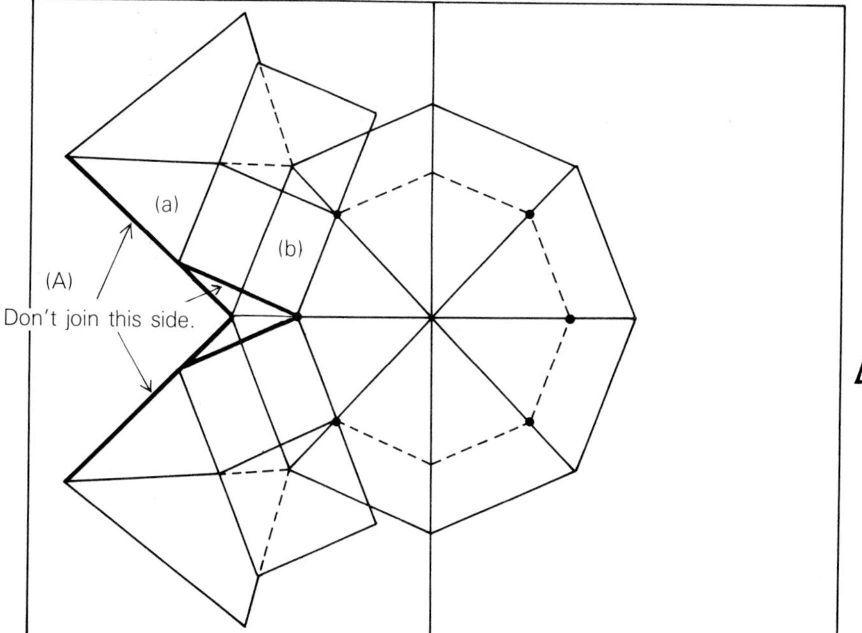

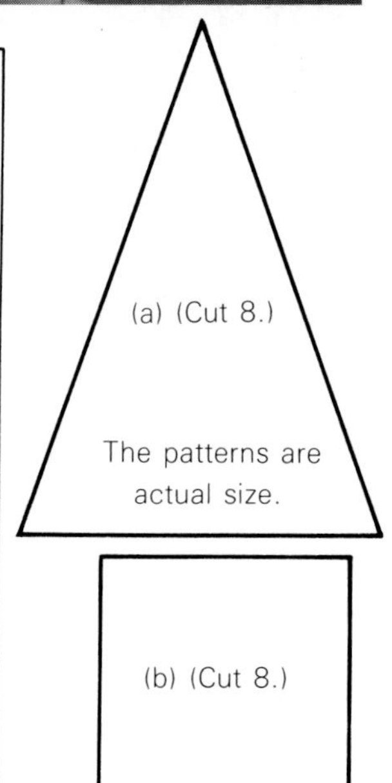

White Ghost Shown on page 7

Cut out 9 pieces of 5 kinds of parts using the patterns below. Join all the pieces together following the diagram at right. The design was inspired by a Japanese folk tale of a badger with a long tongue and a tale of a huge monster. Join the upper parts of (b) and (c) together with Japanese rice paper and glue (a) onto (b). Attach the joined ghost onto the base with pieces of thread at each of the dots as shown.

The patterns are actual size.

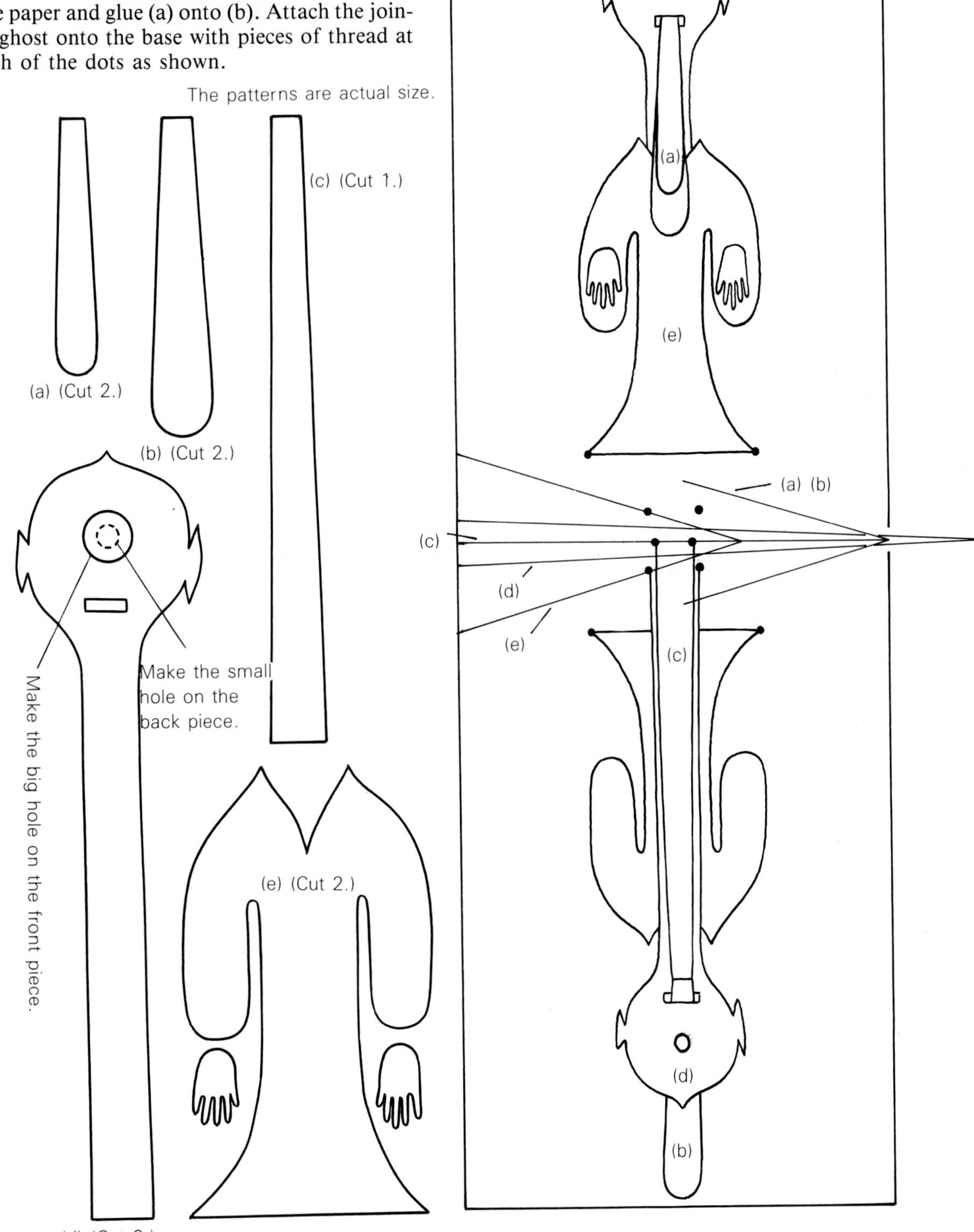

Pond Lily Shown on page 7

Cut out 18 pieces of 9 parts using the patterns below. Join the parts (a) and (b), and (c) and (d) individually with Japanese rice paper. Make two pairs each. Do not join (b) and (c). Join the parts (g) and (f), and (h) and (i) with Japanese rice paper in same manner.

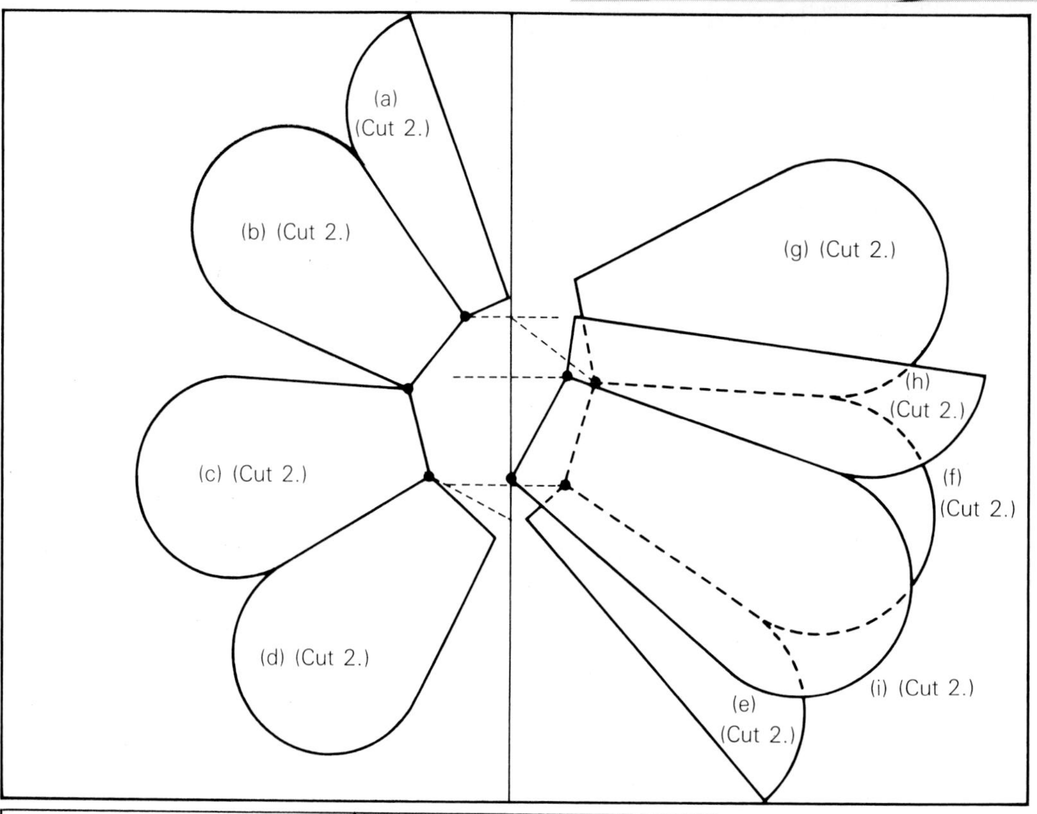

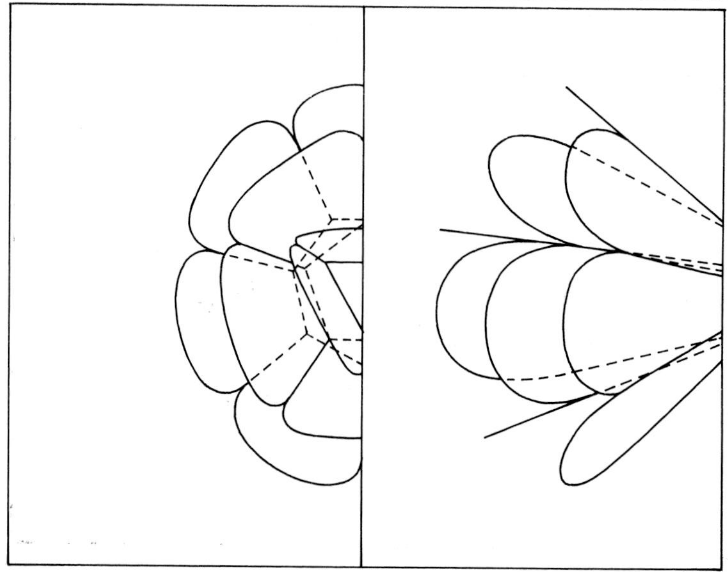

Attach the finished flower onto the base with pieces of thread at each of the dots as shown. Cut another set of the parts for backing in order to hide the joints for a neater finish.

The patterns are seven-tenths actual size.

Weathercock Shown on page 8

Cut out one piece each of 6 parts using the patterns below. It is advisable to cut two pieces each of (a) and (b) for reinforcement.

This pattern is seven-tenths actual size.

Following the diagram, join the parts together. Join the parts (c), (d), (e) and (f) together with Japanese rice paper glued onto the reverse side. Attach the finished weathercock onto the base with pieces of thread at each of 4 dots as shown.

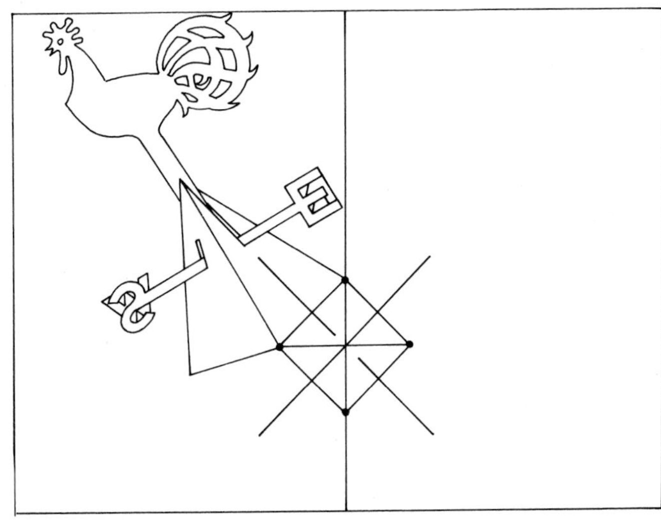

Glass Gallery Shown on page 9

Cut out 14 pieces of 8 kinds of parts using the patterns below. Following the diagram, join the parts together. Glue Japanese rice paper onto the reverse side of the joints of (g) and (h). Attach the finished gallery onto the base with pieces of thread at each of the dots as shown.
The patterns are seven-tenths actual size.

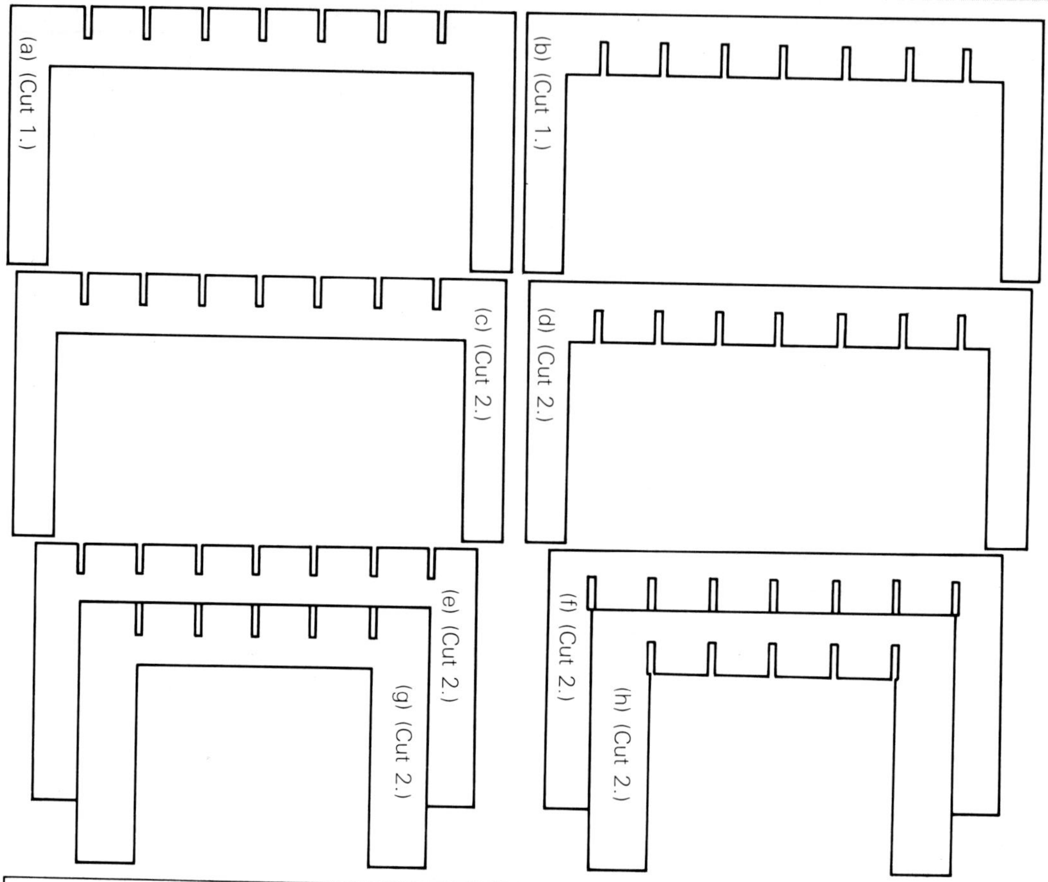

(a) (Cut 1.)

(b) (Cut 1.)

(c) (Cut 2.)

(d) (Cut 2.)

(e) (Cut 2.)

(g) (Cut 2.)

(f) (Cut 2.)

(h) (Cut 2.)

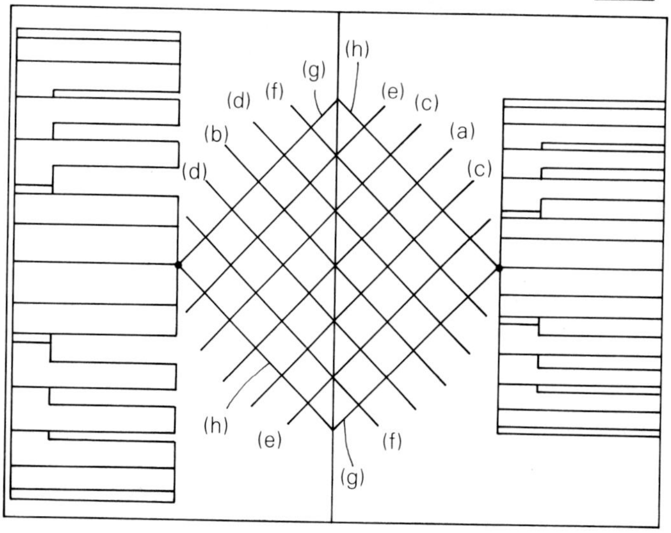

(h) (g) (f) (e) (d) (c) (b) (a) (d) (c) (h) (e) (f) (g)

Tower of Babel Shown on page 10

Cut out one piece each of 14 parts using the patterns below. Following the diagram, join the parts (a) and (b), (c) and (d), (e) and (f), (g) and (h), (i) and (j), (k) and (l), and (m) and (n) individually with Japanese rice paper. Do not join the sides of (b) and (c), (d) and (e), (f) and (g), (h) and (i), (j) and (k), and (l) and (m).
Attach the finished tower onto the base with thread.
The patterns are seven-tenths actual size.

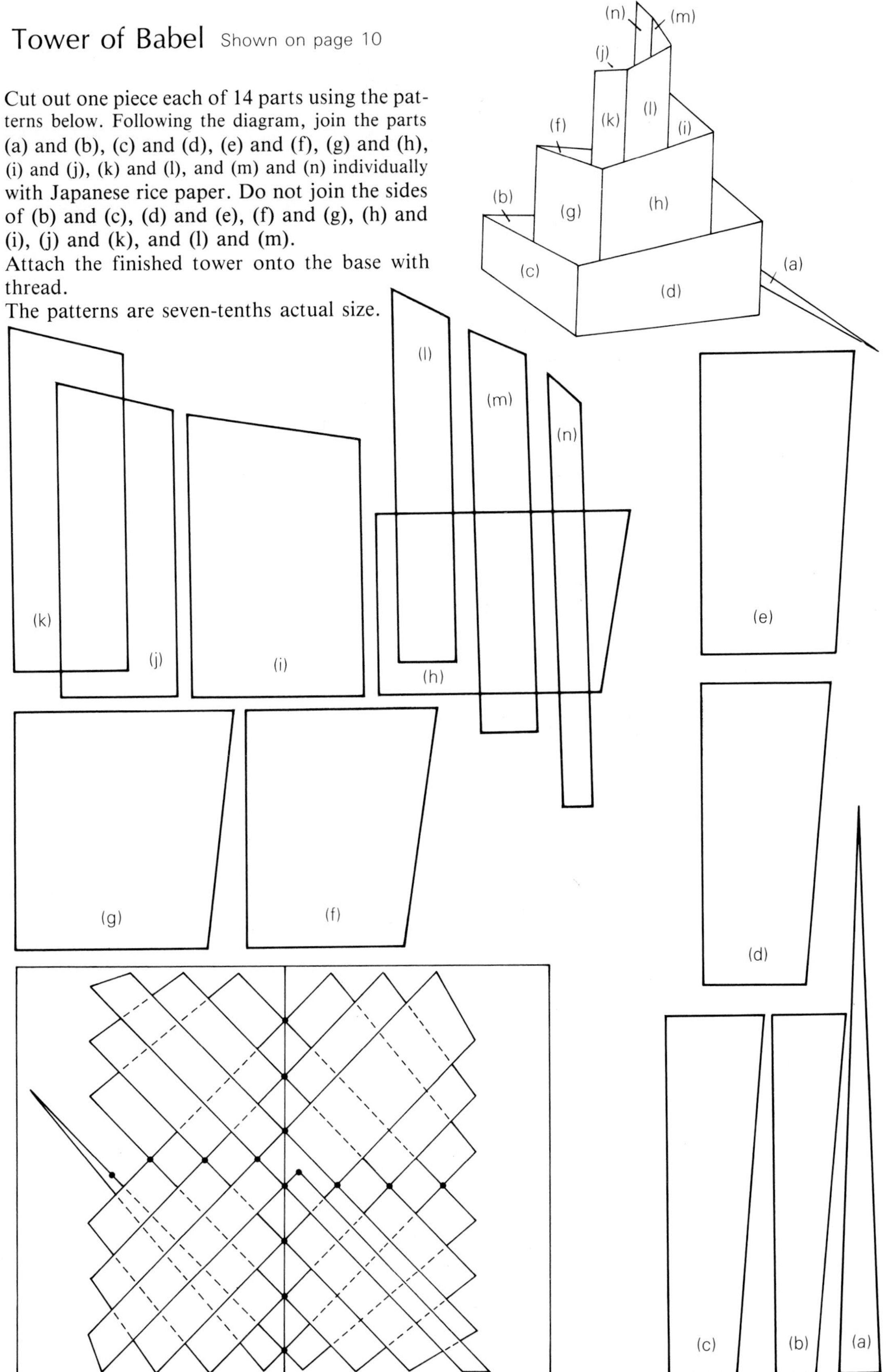

Noh Stage Shown on page 12

Cut out 20 pieces of 6 kinds of parts using the patterns below. Join them together, following the diagram. Attach the stage onto the base with thread.

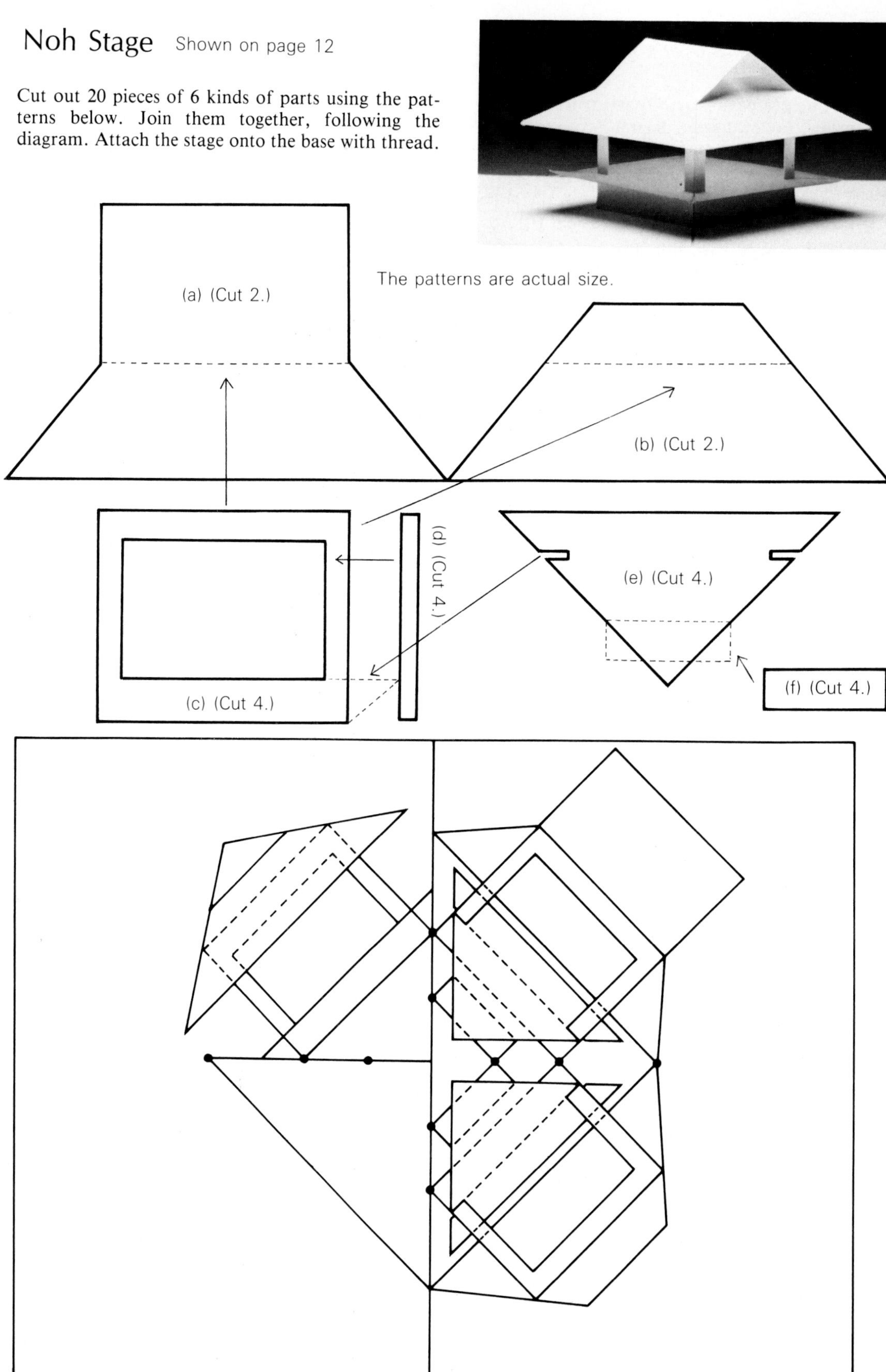

Vase Shown on page 14

Cut out 6 pieces of 3 kinds of parts using the patterns below. Following the diagram, join the parts (a) and (b), and (b) and (c) with Japanese rice paper glued on the reverse side. Join another set. Join two sets together with Japanese rice paper. Attach the joined piece onto the base with thread.
In order to hide the joints, cut 6 more pieces for backing for a neater finish.

(a) (Cut 2.)

(b) (Cut 2.)

(c) (Cut 2.)

The patterns are actual size.

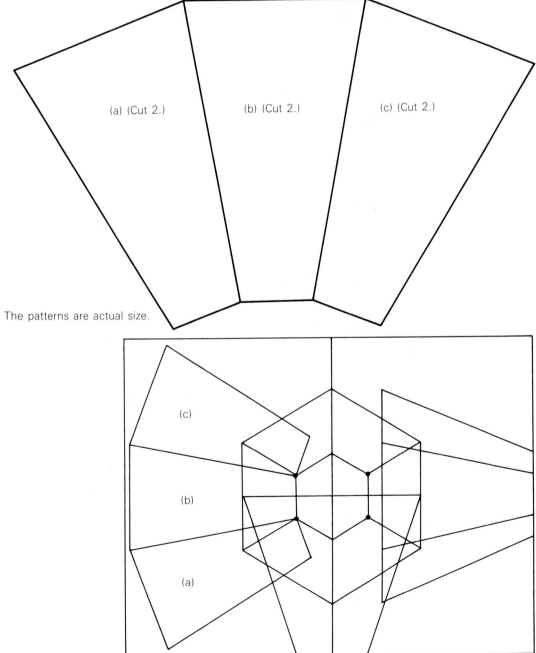

(c)

(b)

(a)

Globe Shown on page 15

Cut out 16 pieces of 8 kinds of parts using the patterns below. Join the parts (a) and (b) first and then (c) and (d), (f) and (e), and (g) and (h) to form a ball. The patterns are eight-tenths actual size.

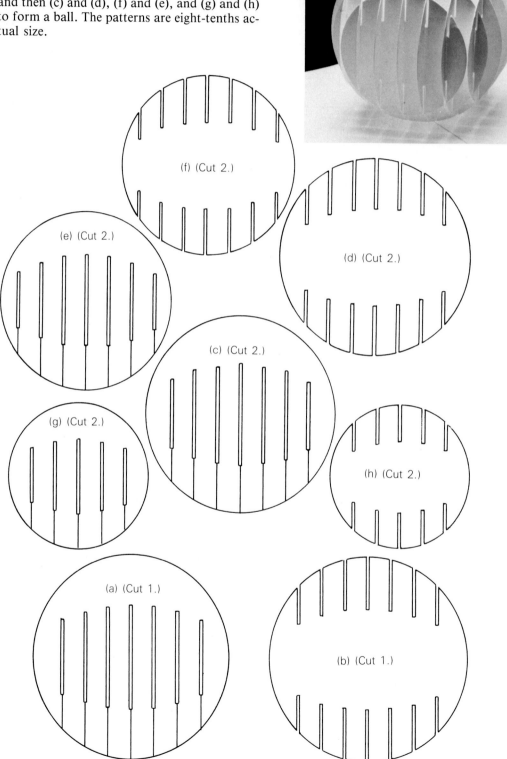

(f) (Cut 2.)

(e) (Cut 2.)

(d) (Cut 2.)

(c) (Cut 2.)

(g) (Cut 2.)

(h) (Cut 2.)

(a) (Cut 1.)

(b) (Cut 1.)

Attach the joined ball onto the base with thread.

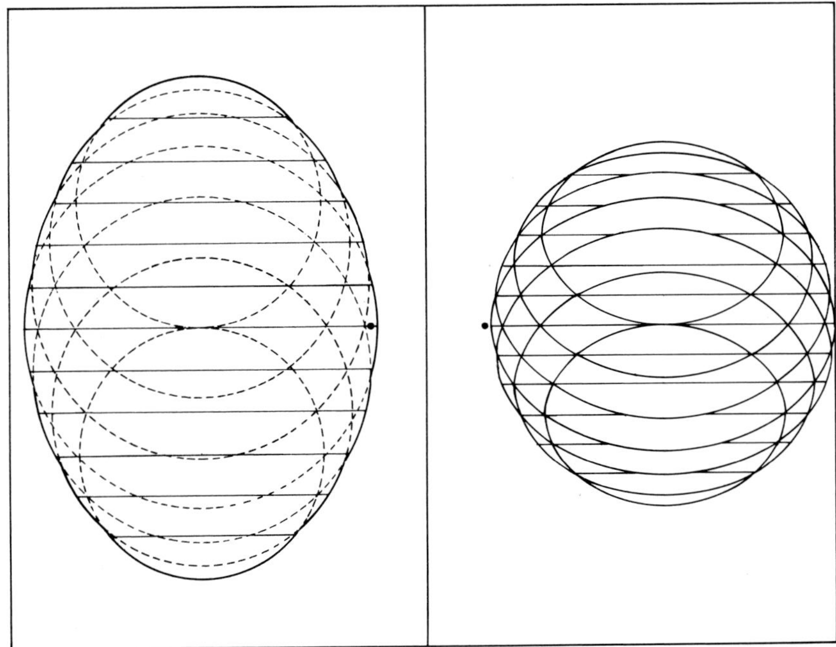

Yacht Shown on page 15

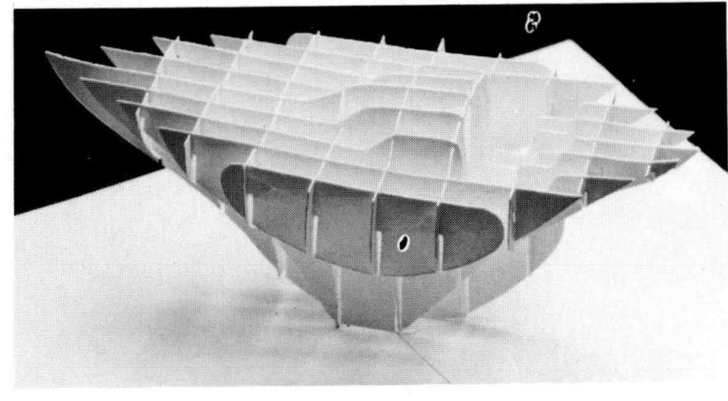

The patterns (all eight-tenths actual size) are shown on the next page. Cut out 18 pieces of 14 kinds of parts from (a) to (n). Start joining with the biggest parts (a) and (f), then join horizontally and vertically ending with (i) and (n). Attach the joined yacht onto the base with thread. Two pieces of thread which are inserted into the holes on the center line should be left 1 cm free on the front.

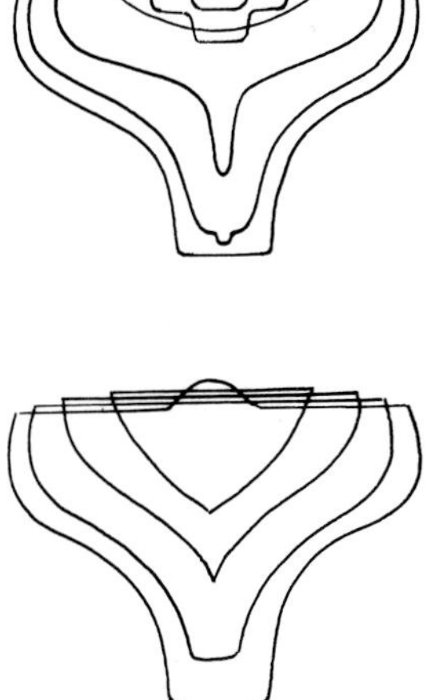

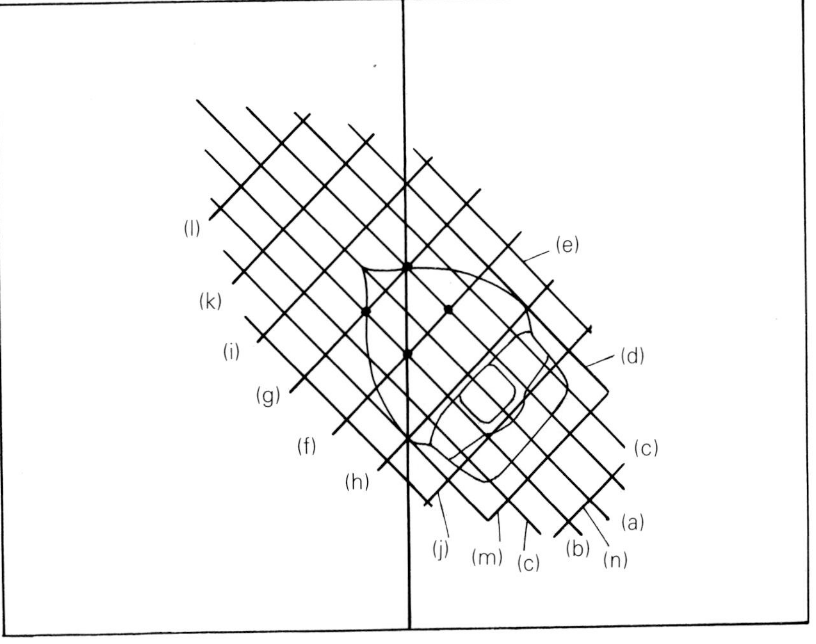

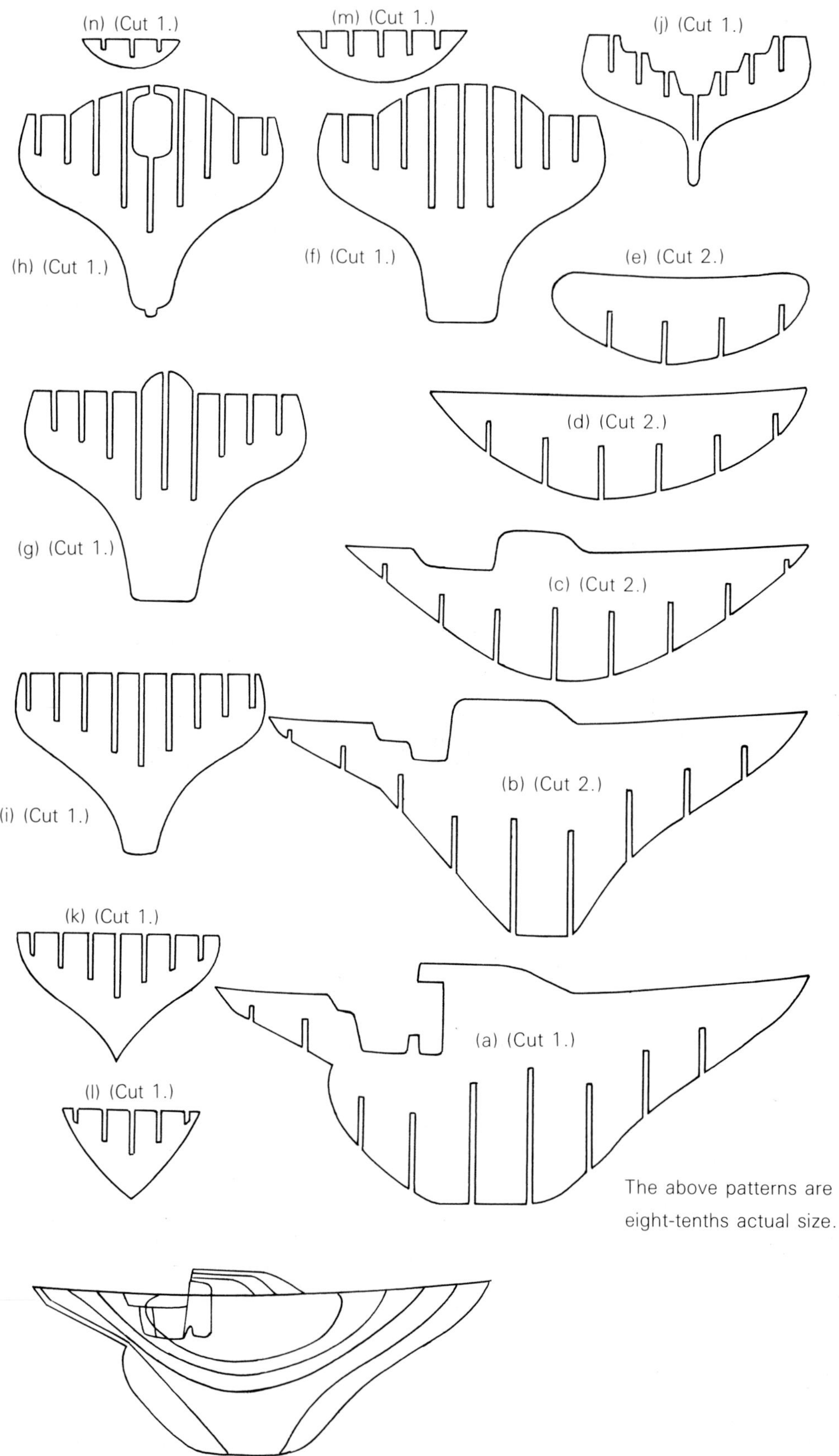

The above patterns are eight-tenths actual size.

● The actual-size patterns for 0° and 90° open types

Block

Shown on page 6

● Key for the lines

————	Cutting line
— — — —	Valley fold line
- - - - - -	Ridge fold line

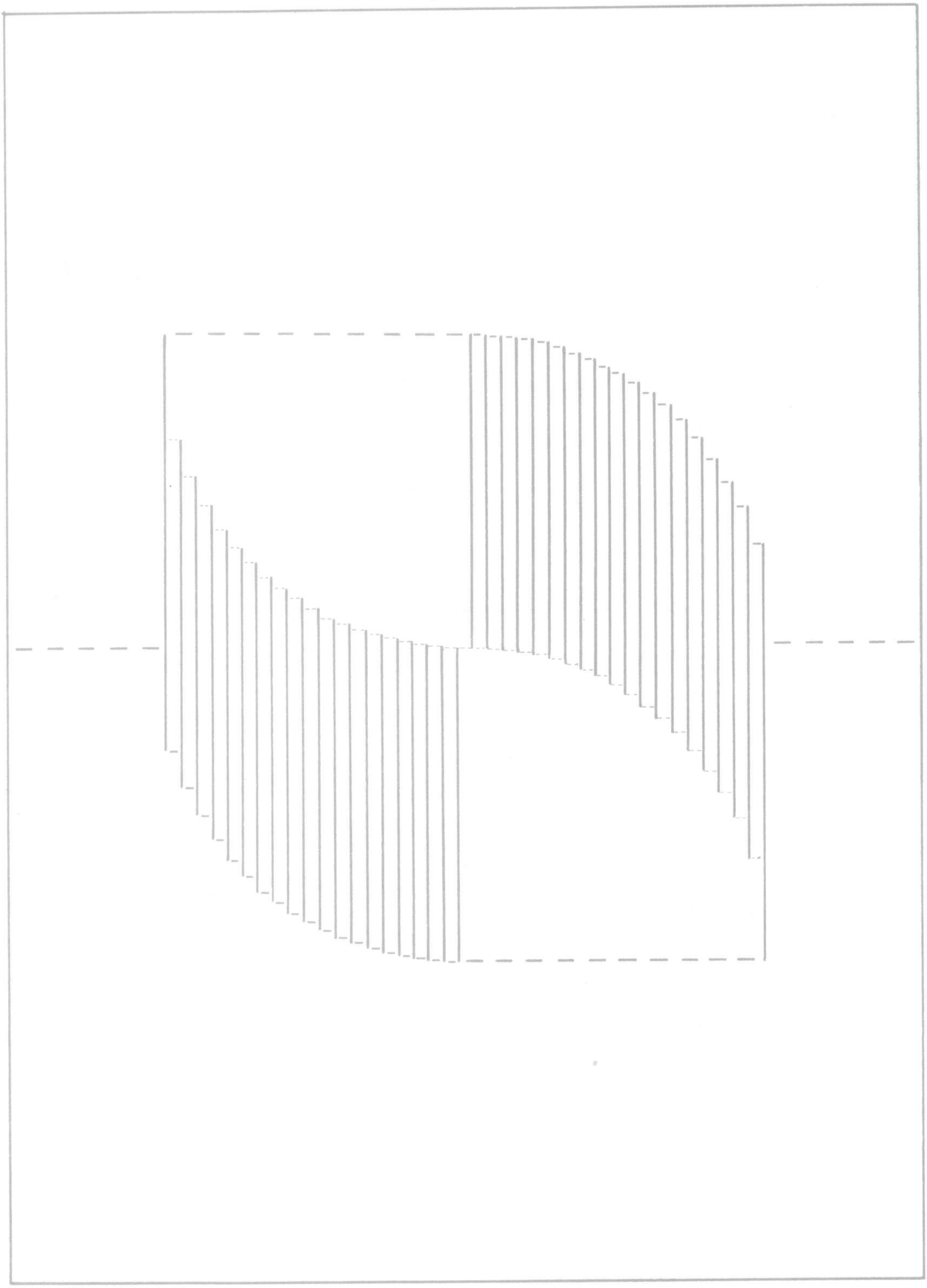

Japanese Dolls Shown on page 8

● key for the lines

———— Cutting line

— — — — Valley fold line

- - - - - - Ridge fold line

Mouse Shown on page 8

● key for the lines

——— Cutting line

– – – – Valley fold line

- - - - - Ridge fold line

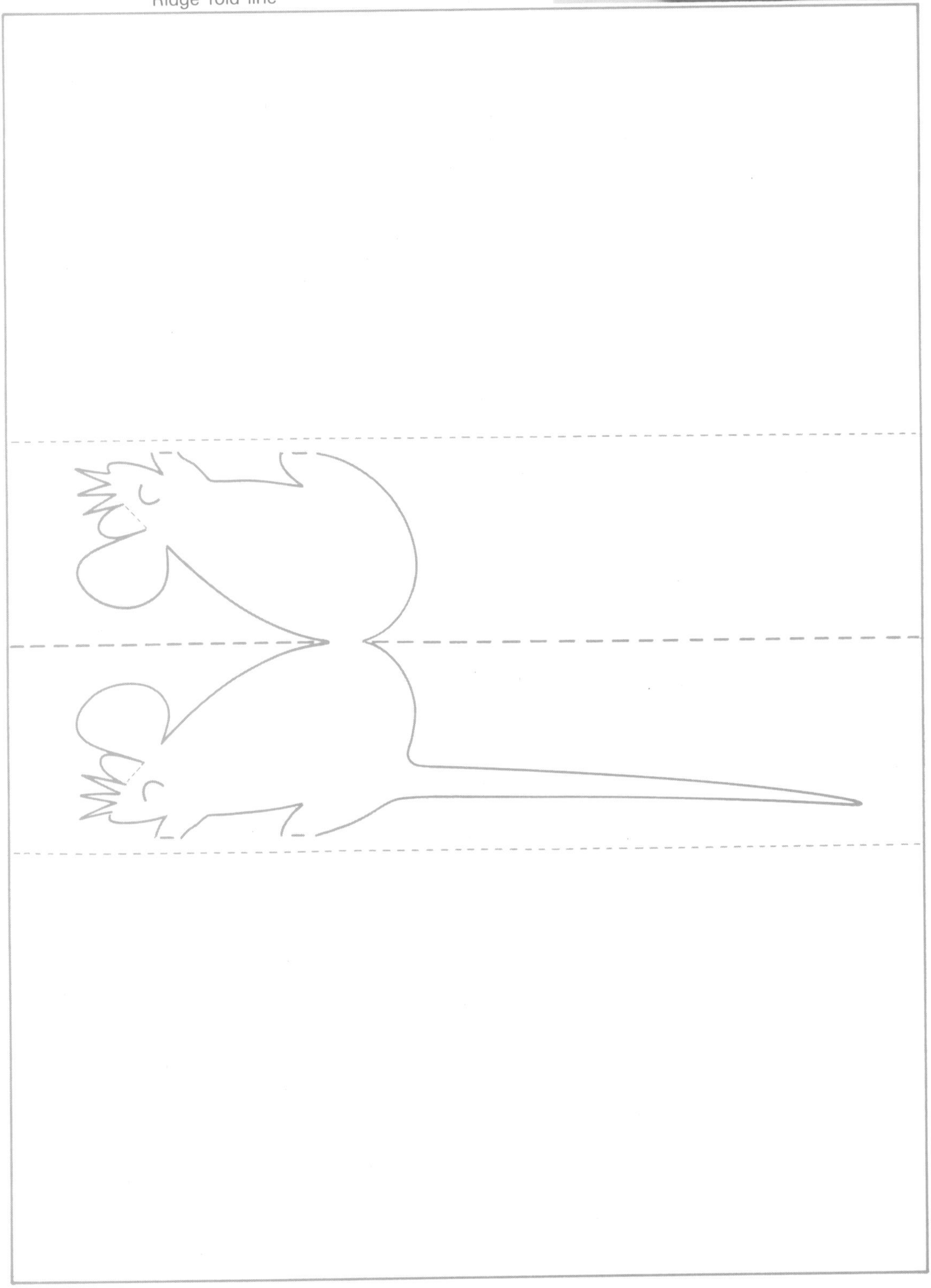

Open-air Theater Shown on page 10

● key for the lines

——————— Cutting line

— — — — — — Valley fold line

- - - - - - - - - - - Ridge fold line

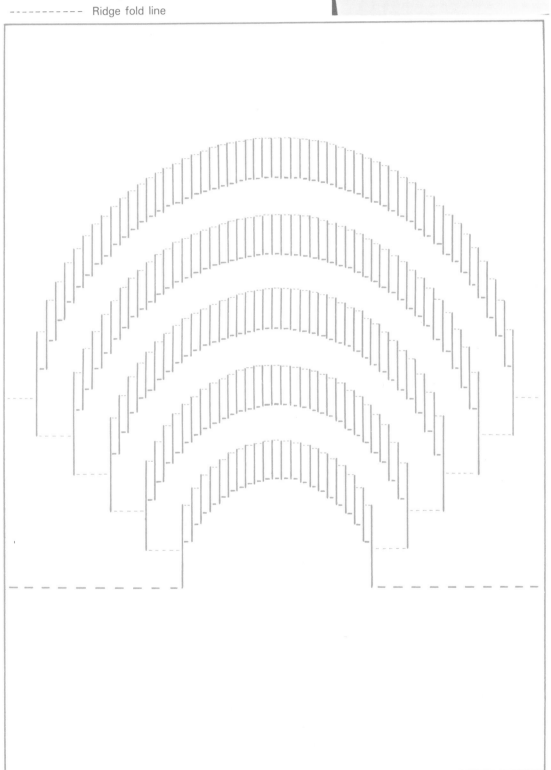

White Chapel Shown on page 11

● key for the lines

——————— Cutting line

– – – – – – – Valley fold line

- - - - - - - - - - - Ridge fold line

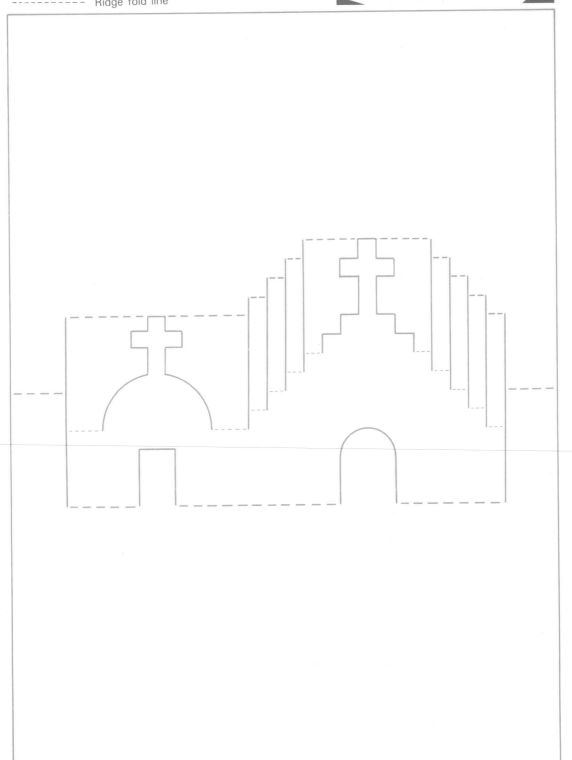

Castle Shown on page 11

Shown on page 11

● key for the lines

- Cutting line
- Valley fold line
- Ridge fold line

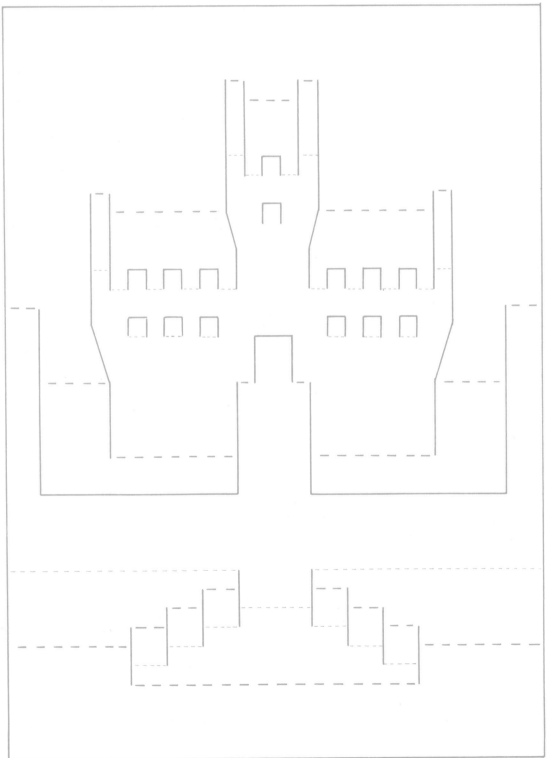

Music Shell Shown on page 13

● key for the lines

Cutting line

Valley fold line

Ridge fold line

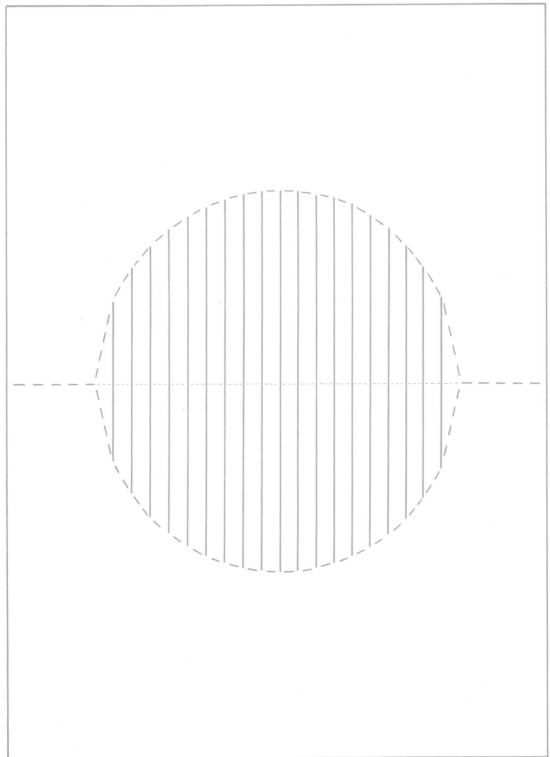

Grade Separation Shown on page 13

● key for the lines

———————— Cutting line

— — — — — — Valley fold line

- - - - - - - - - - - Ridge fold line

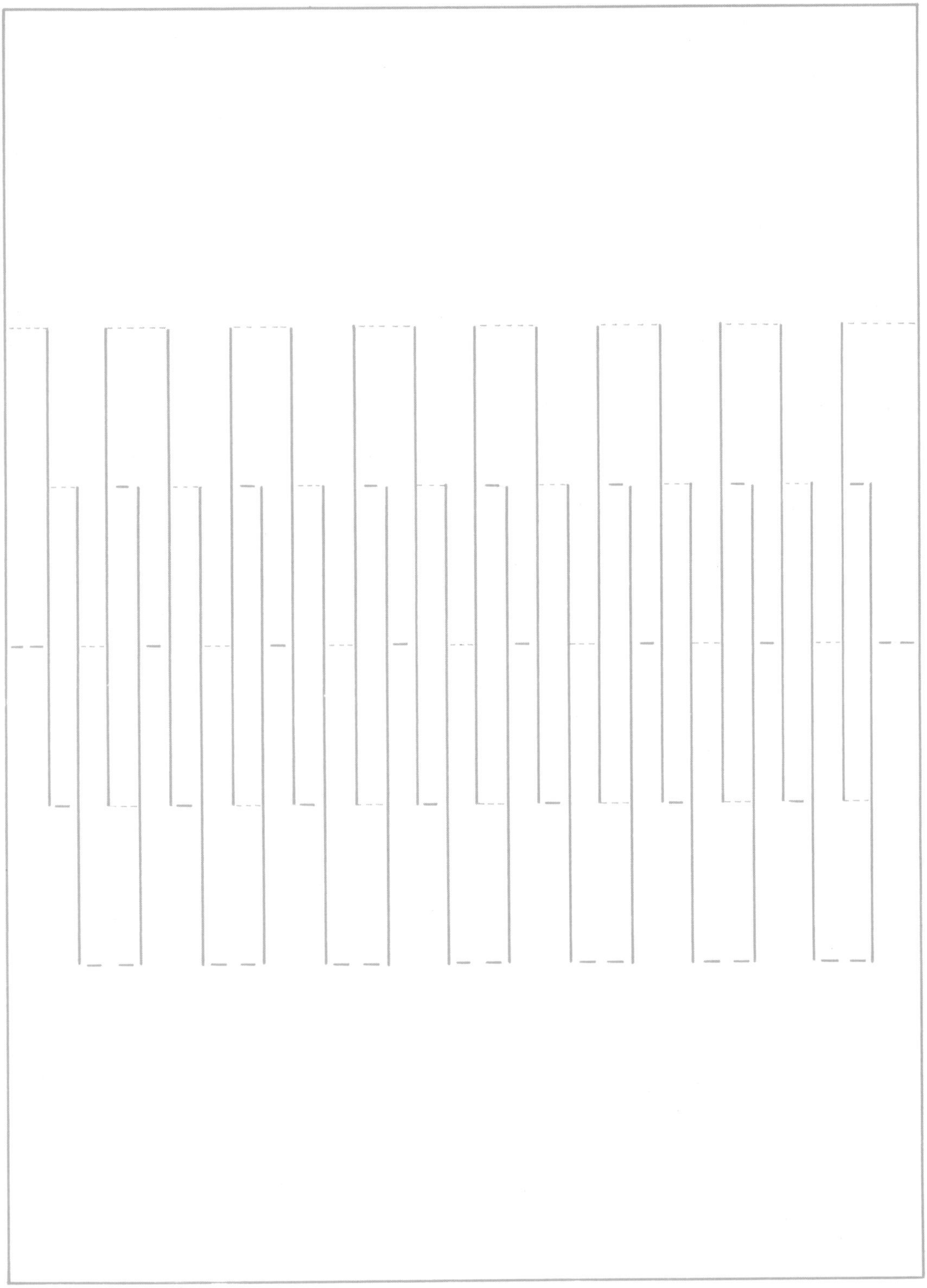

Decoration Shown on page 14

● key for the lines

——————— Cutting line

— — — — — — Valley fold line

- - - - - - - - - - - Ridge fold line

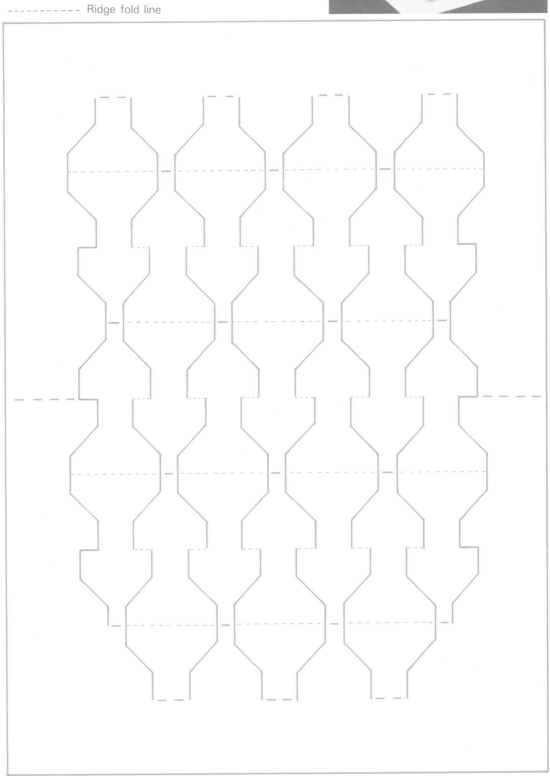

Hippopotamus Shown on page 16

● key for the lines

——— Cutting line

– – – – – – Valley fold line

- - - - - - - - Ridge fold line

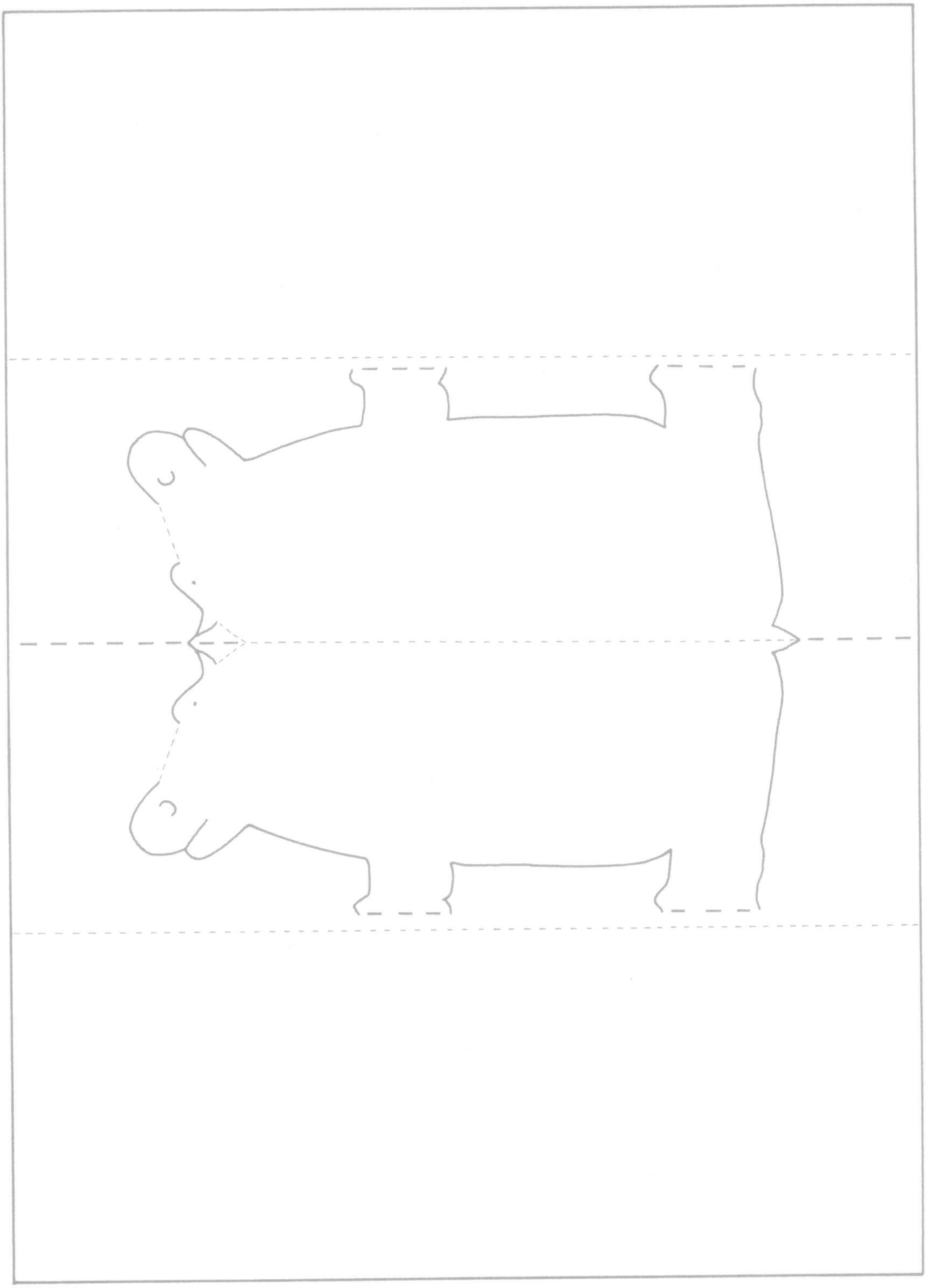

Lamb Shown on page 16

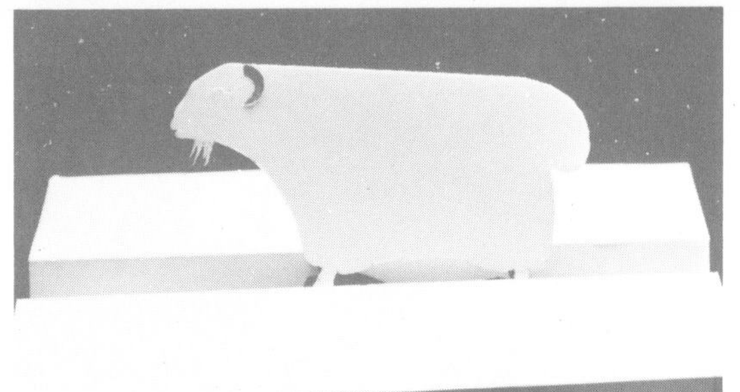

● key for the lines

——————— Cutting line

— — — — — — Valley fold line

- - - - - - - - - - - Ridge fold line

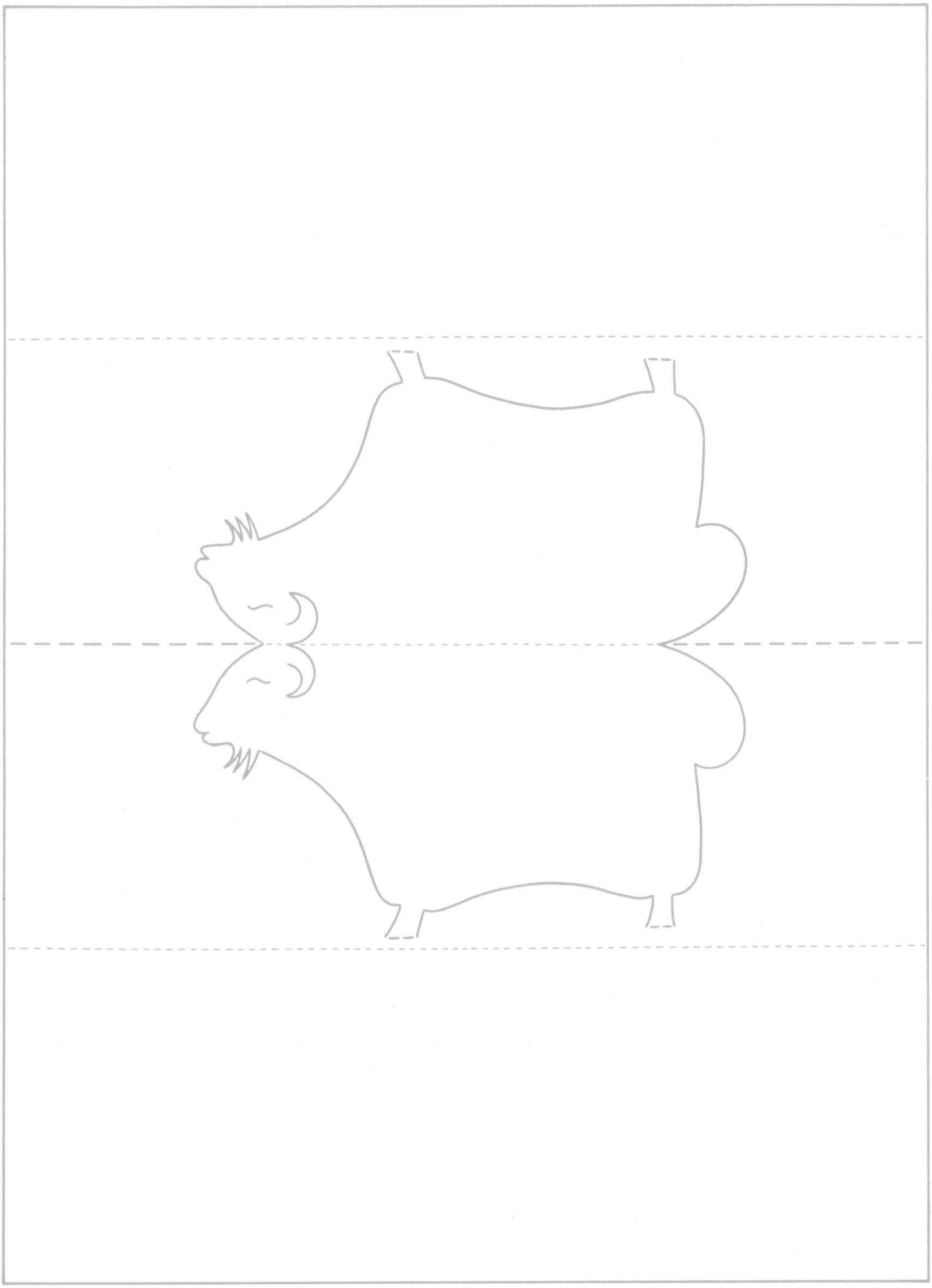

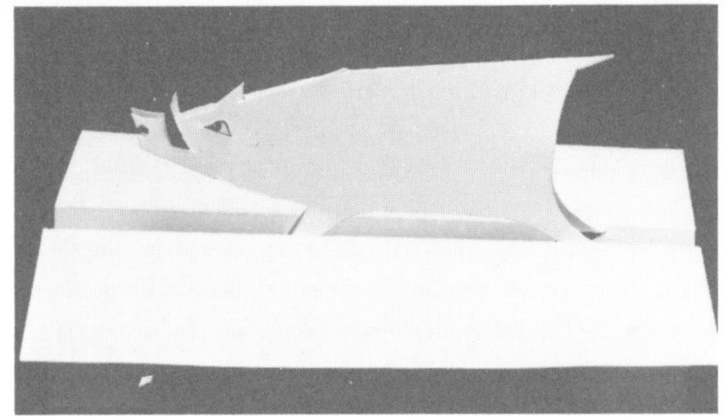

Wild Boar Shown on page 16

● key for the lines

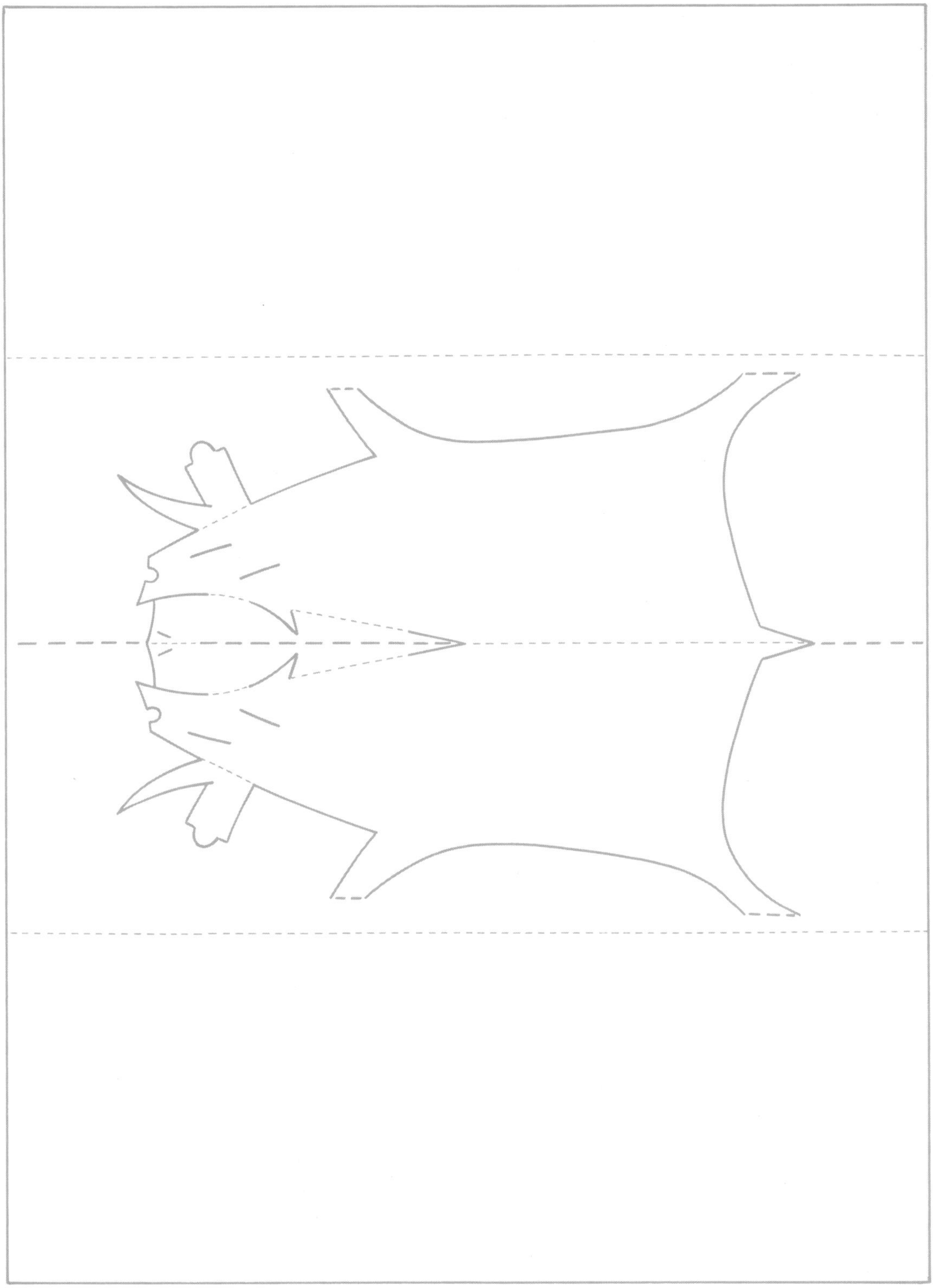

——— Cutting line

– – – – Valley fold line

- - - - - - Ridge fold line

Horse Shown on page 16

● key for the lines

——— Cutting line

– – – – Valley fold line

- - - - - - Ridge fold line

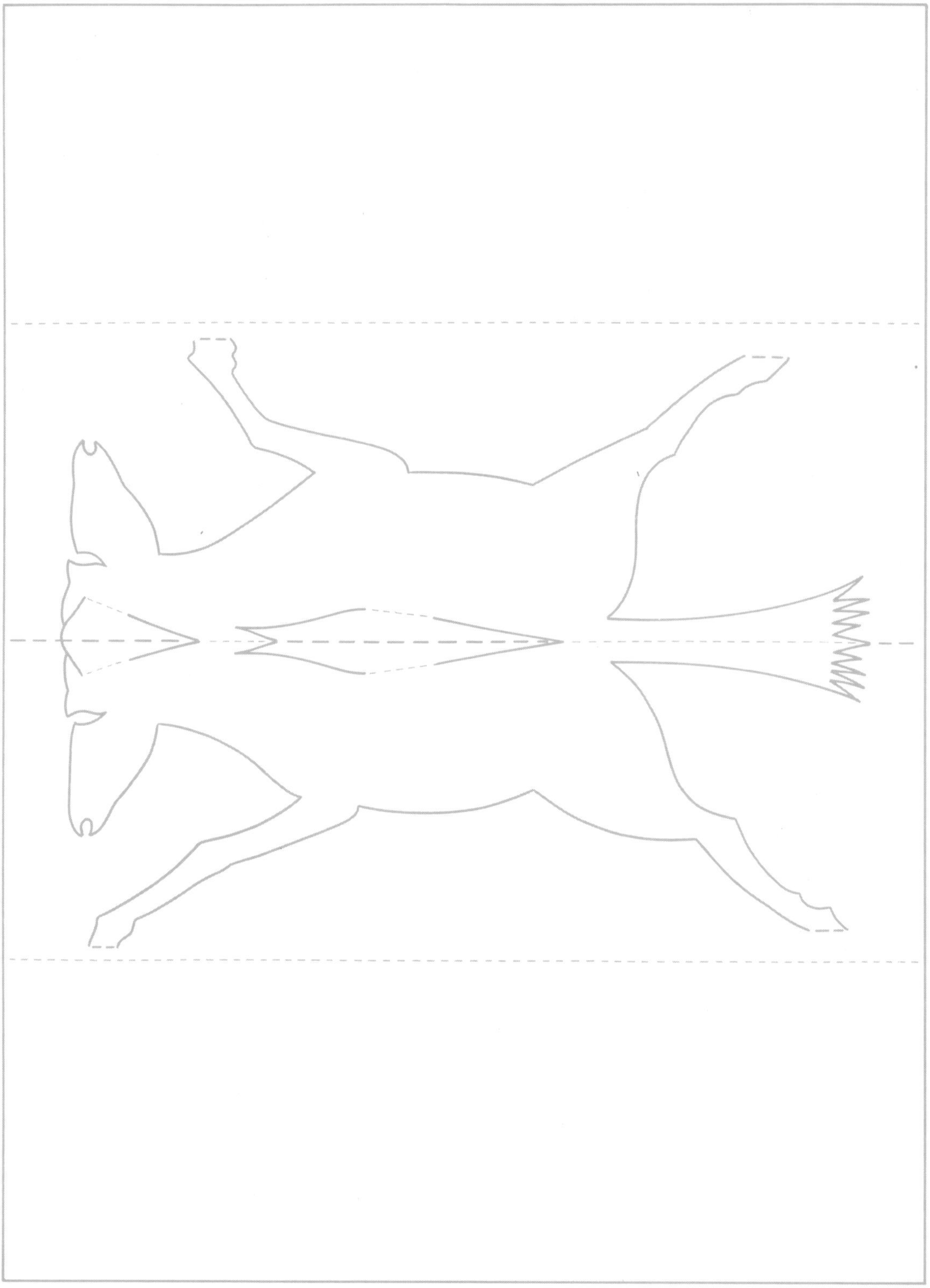

Walrus Shown on page 17

Shown on page 17

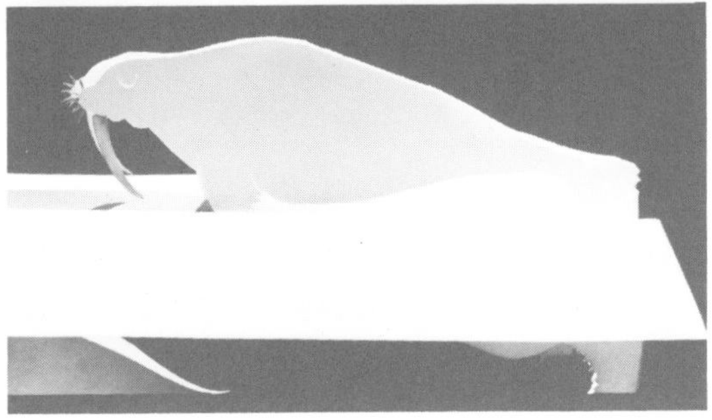

● key for the lines

——— Cutting line

– – – – Valley fold line

- - - - - Ridge fold line

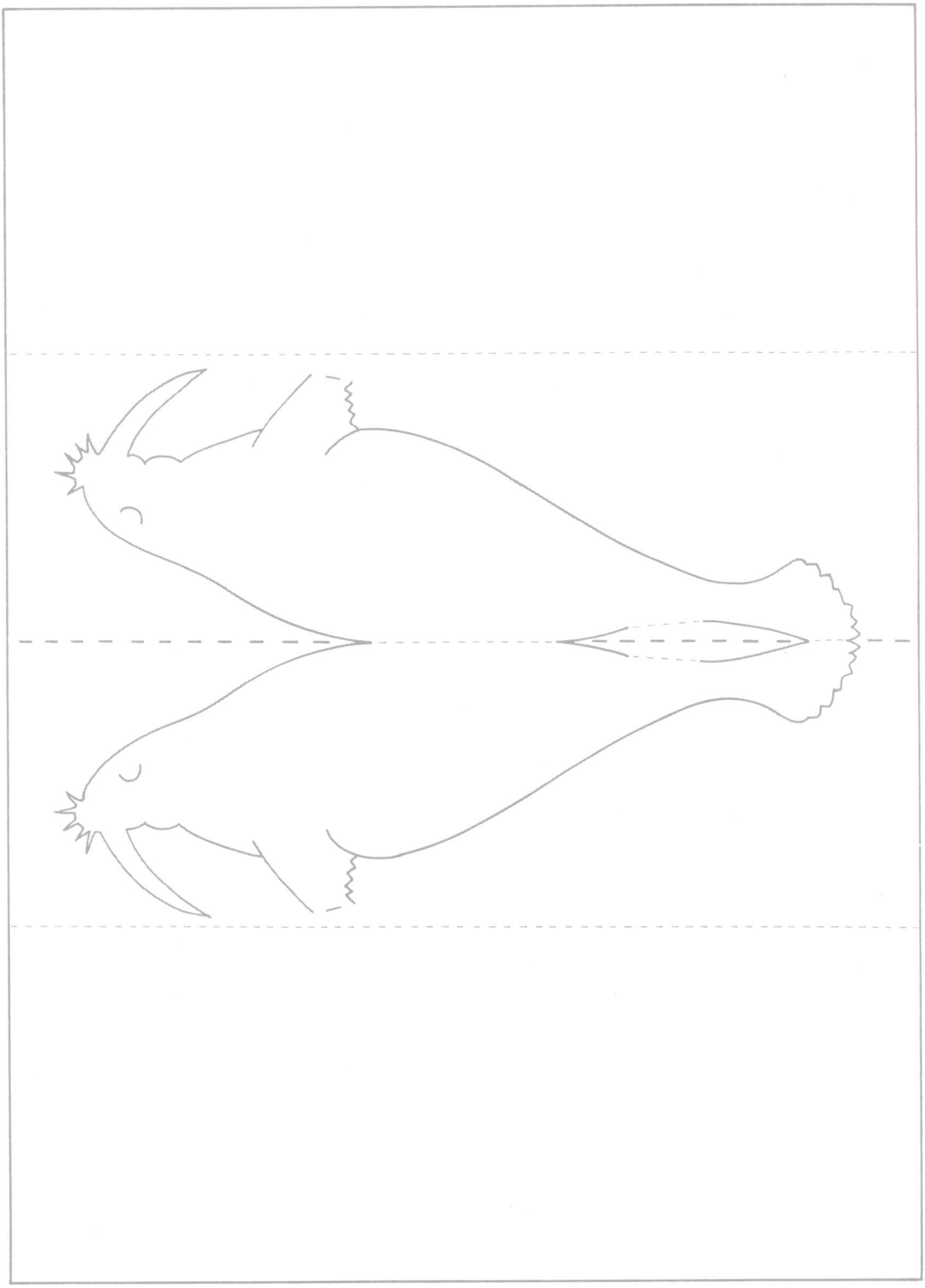

Shark Shown on page 17

● key for the lines

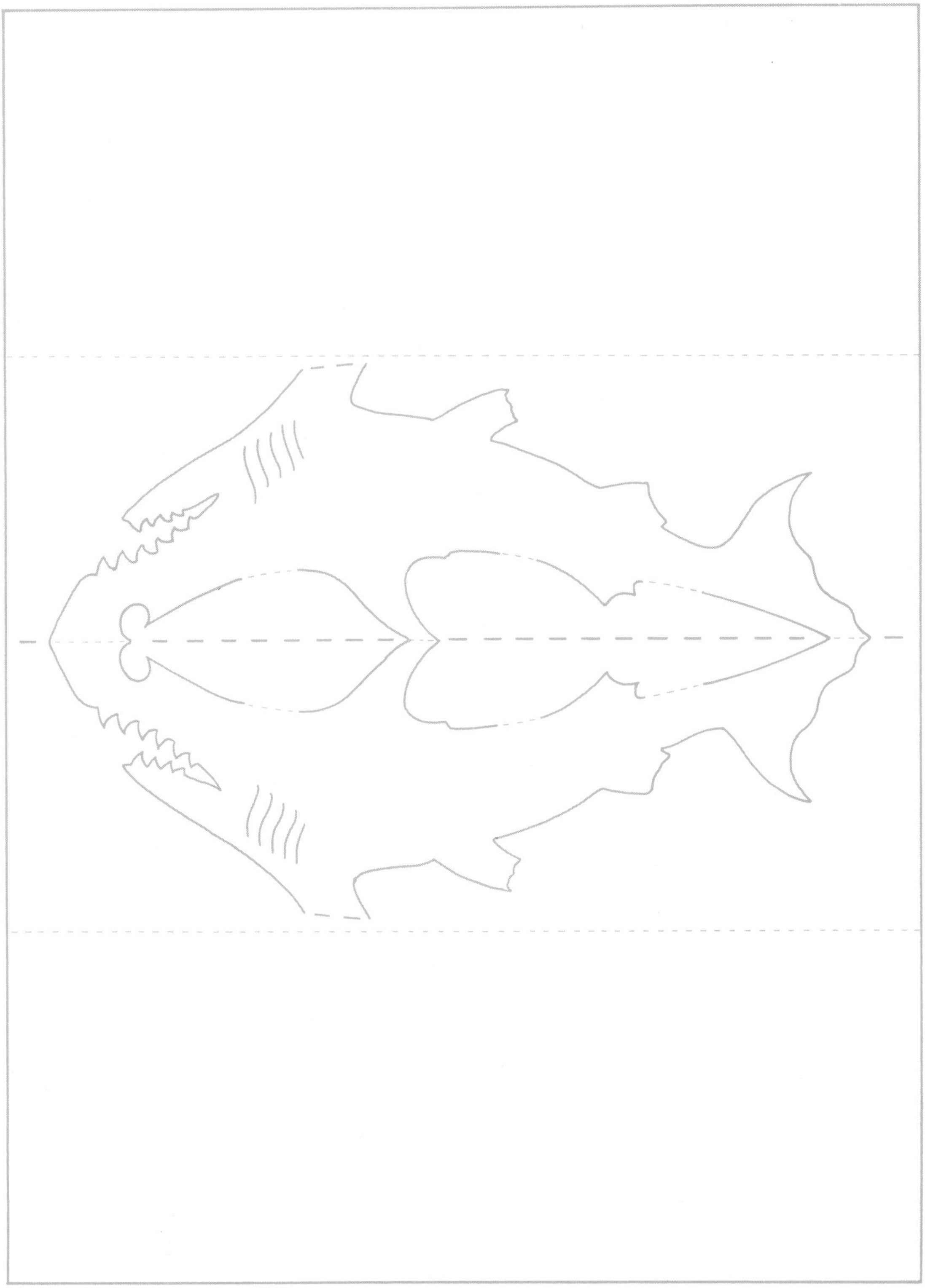

- Cutting line
- Valley fold line
- Ridge fold line

Lion Shown on page 17

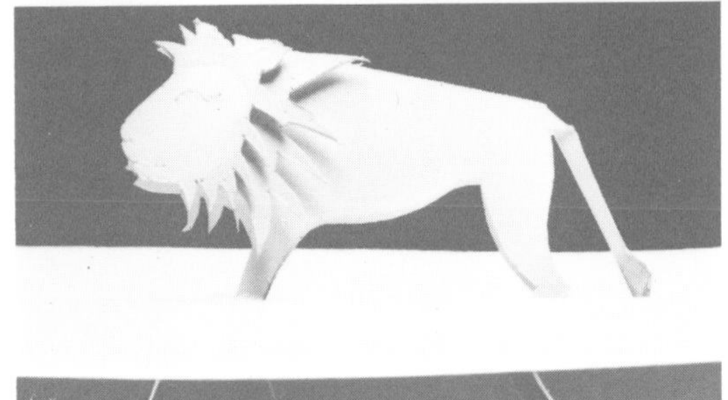

● key for the lines

——— Cutting line

– – – – Valley fold line

- - - - - - Ridge fold line

Little Bear Shown on page 17

● key for the lines

Cutting line

Valley fold line

Ridge fold line

Crab Shown on page 18

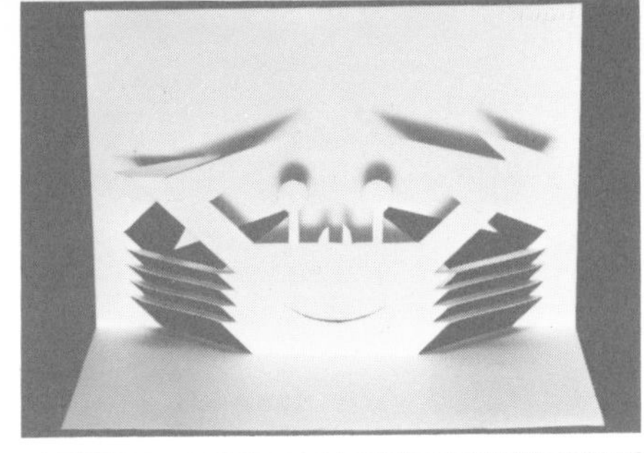

● key for the lines

——— Cutting line

– – – – Valley fold line

- - - - - Ridge fold line

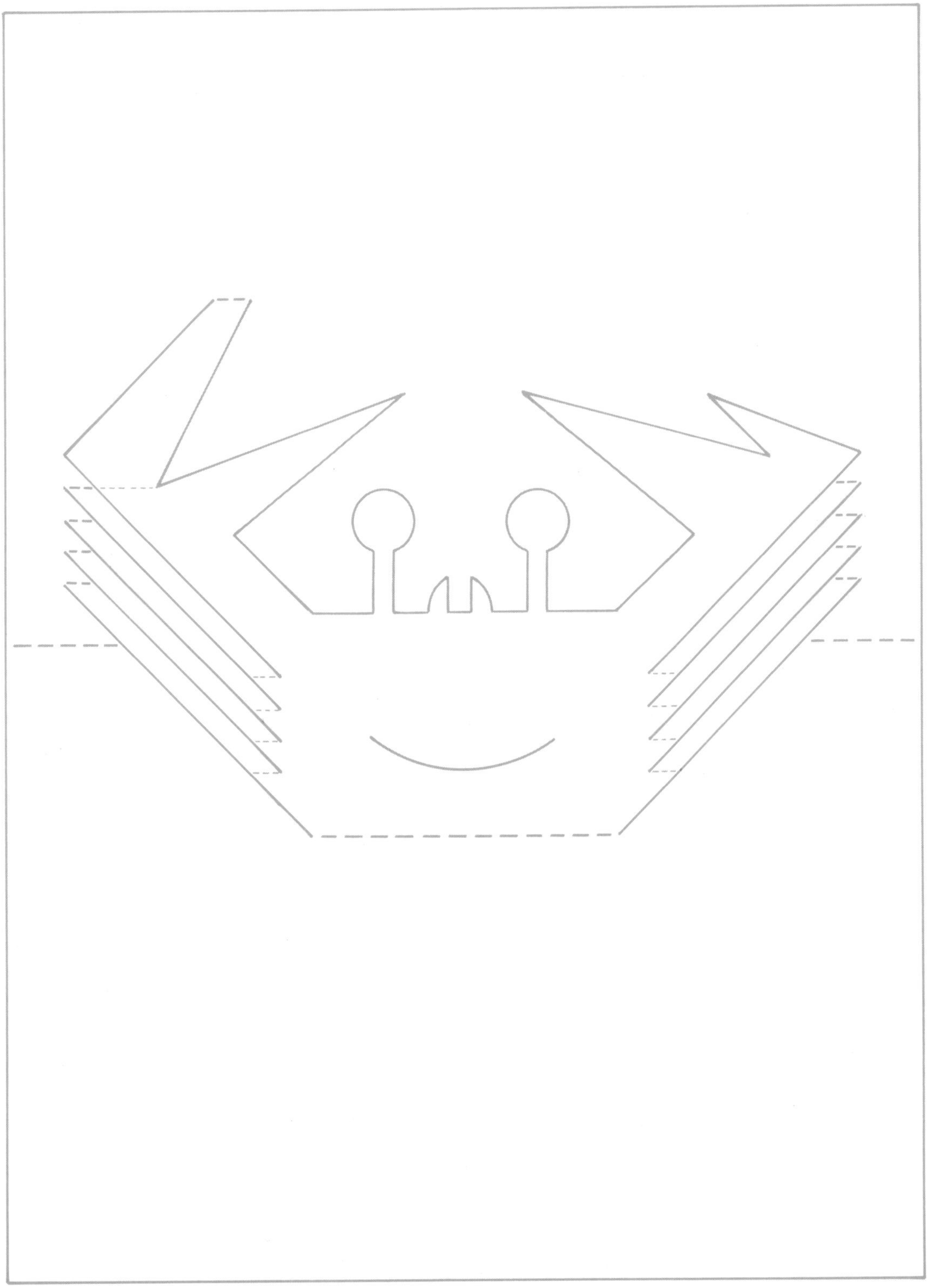

Tortoise Shown on page 18

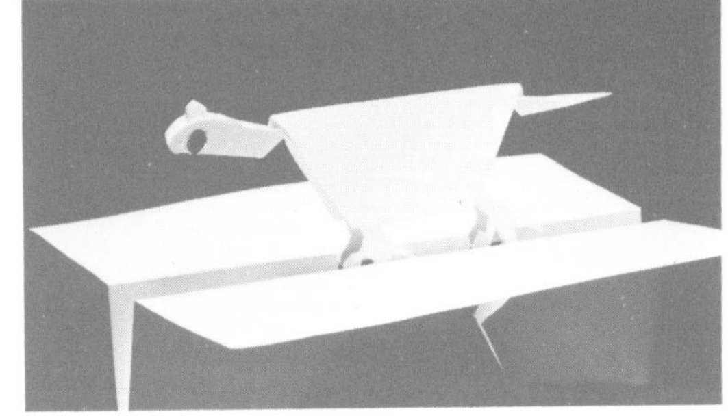

● key for the lines

Cutting line

Valley fold line

Ridge fold line

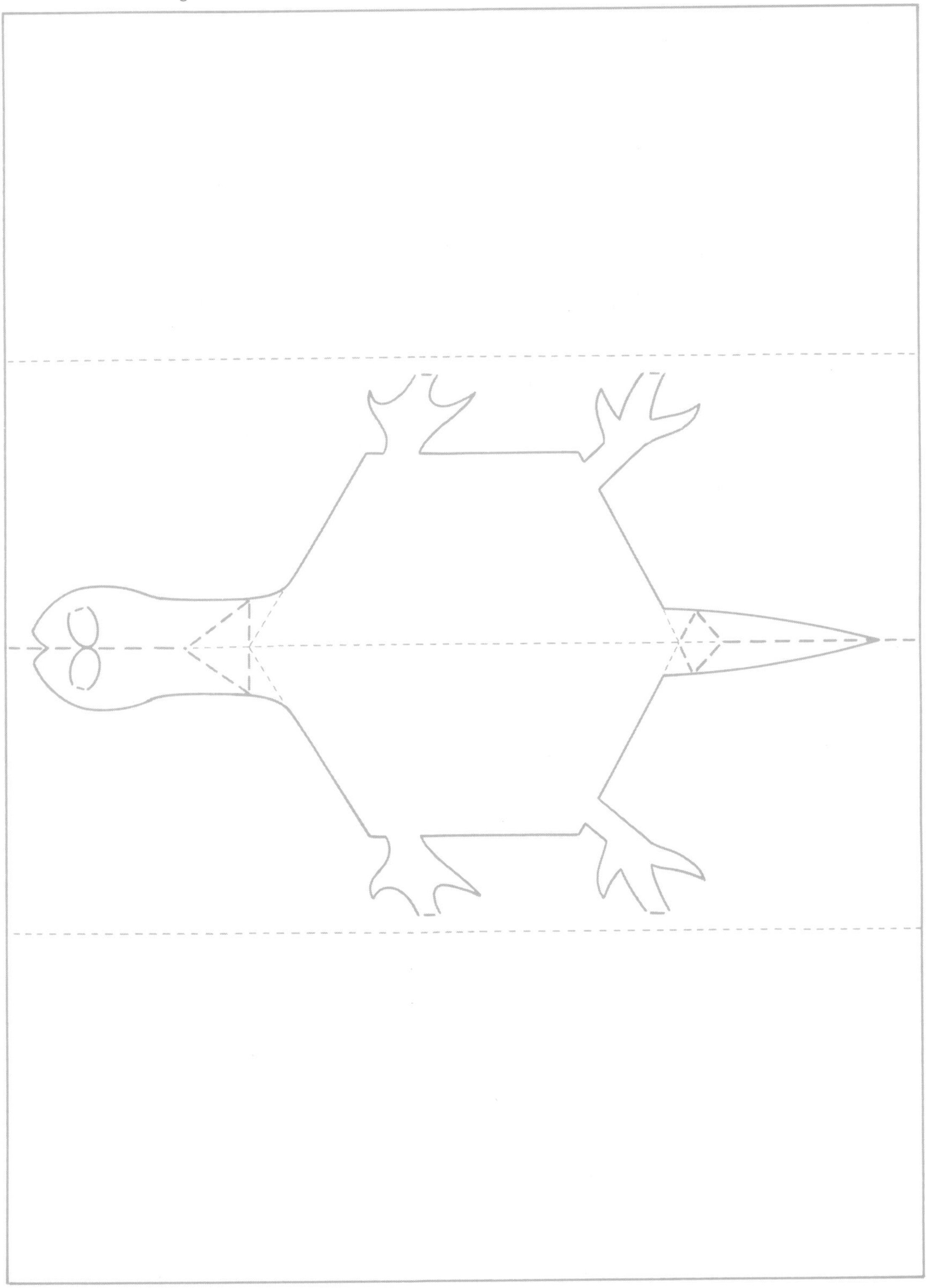

Mask Shown on page 18 (Left)

● key for the lines

——————— Cutting line

– – – – – – Valley fold line

- - - - - - - - - - - Ridge fold line

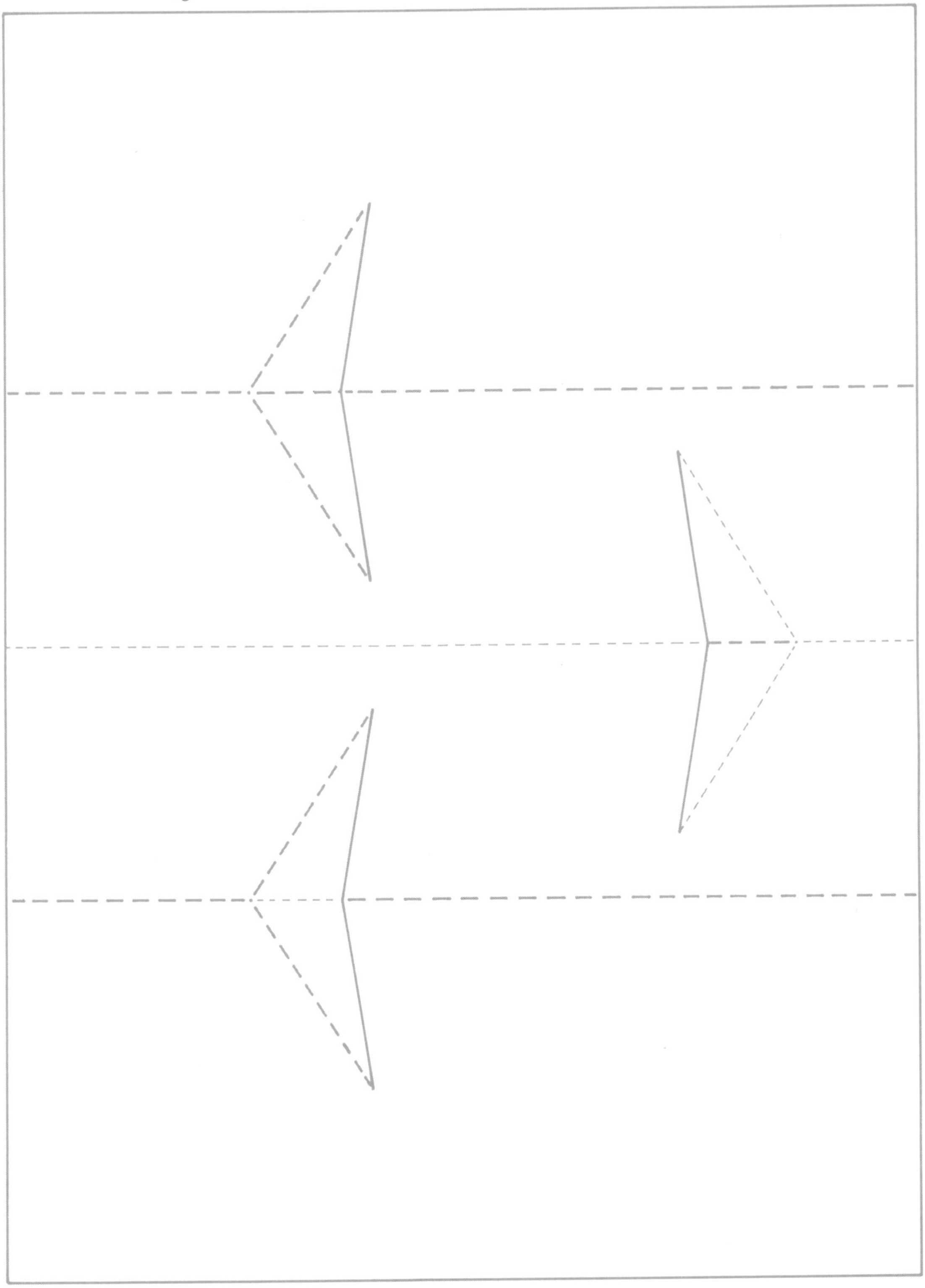

Mask Shown on page 18 (Right)

●key for the lines

——————— Cutting line

– – – – – – Valley fold line

- - - - - - - - - - - Ridge fold line

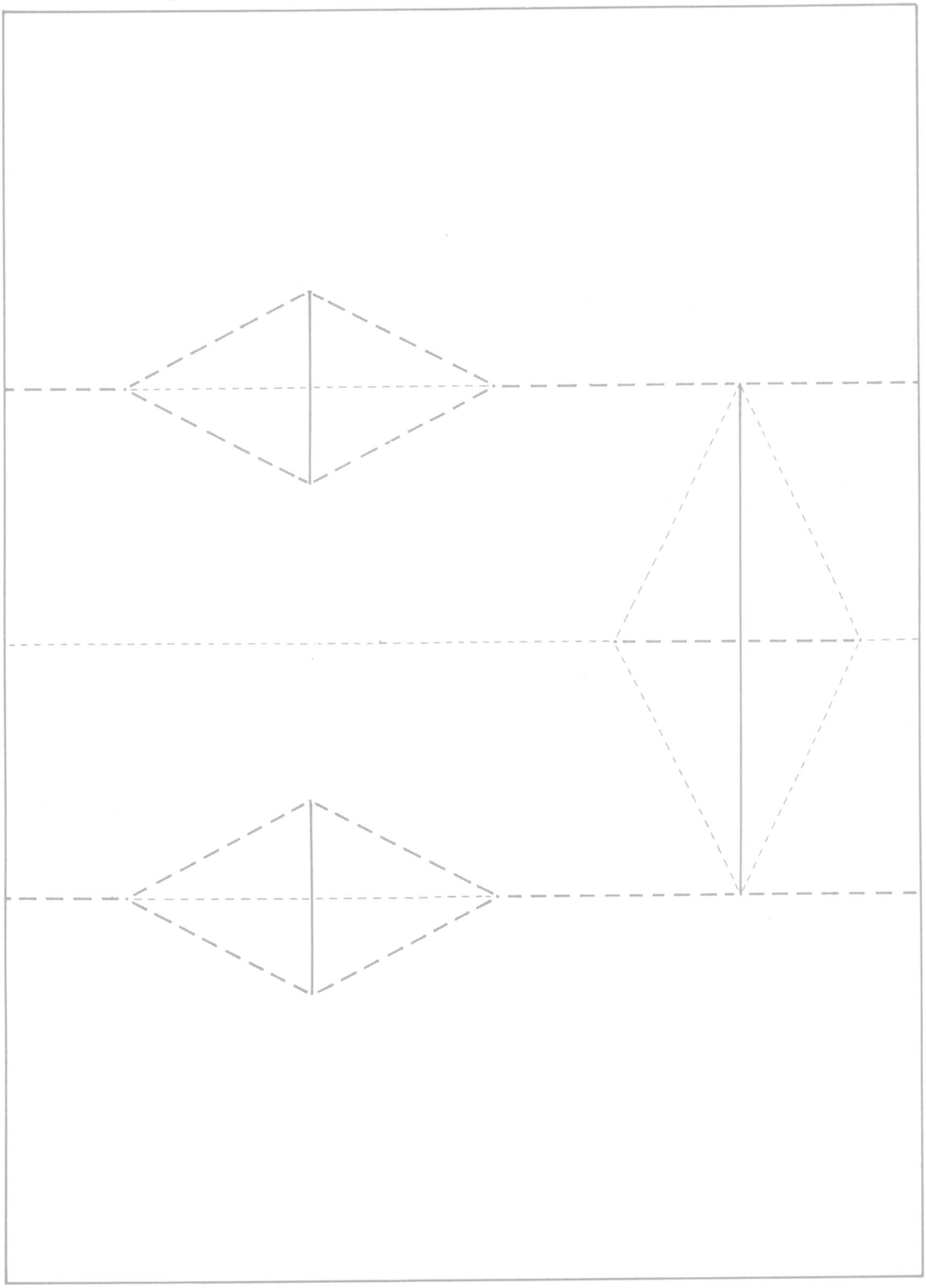

Waterbird Shown on page 19

● key for the lines

——— Cutting line

– – – – – Valley fold line

- - - - - - - Ridge fold line

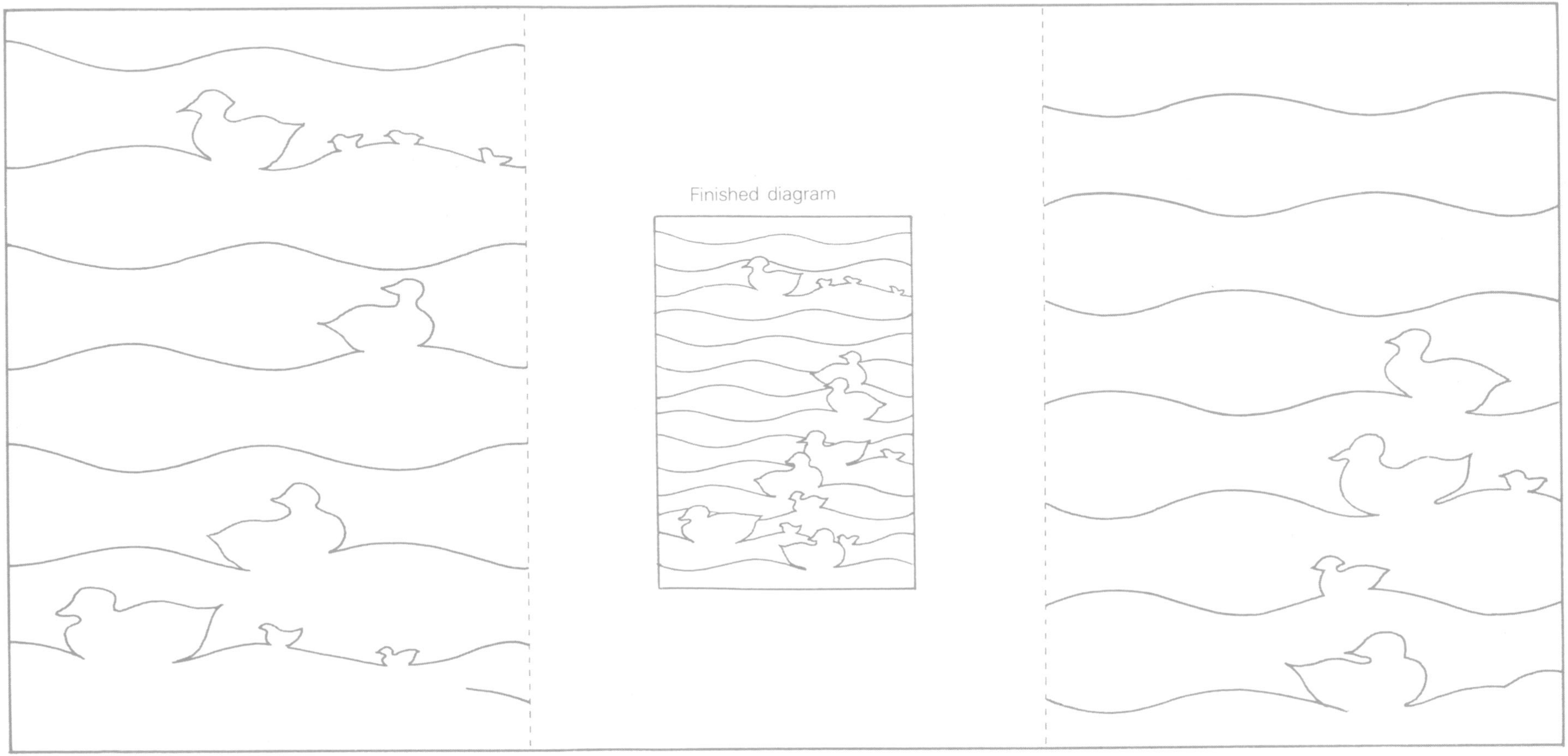

Finished diagram

Offshore Cruising

Shown on page 19

- key for the lines

Cutting line

Valley fold line

Ridge fold line

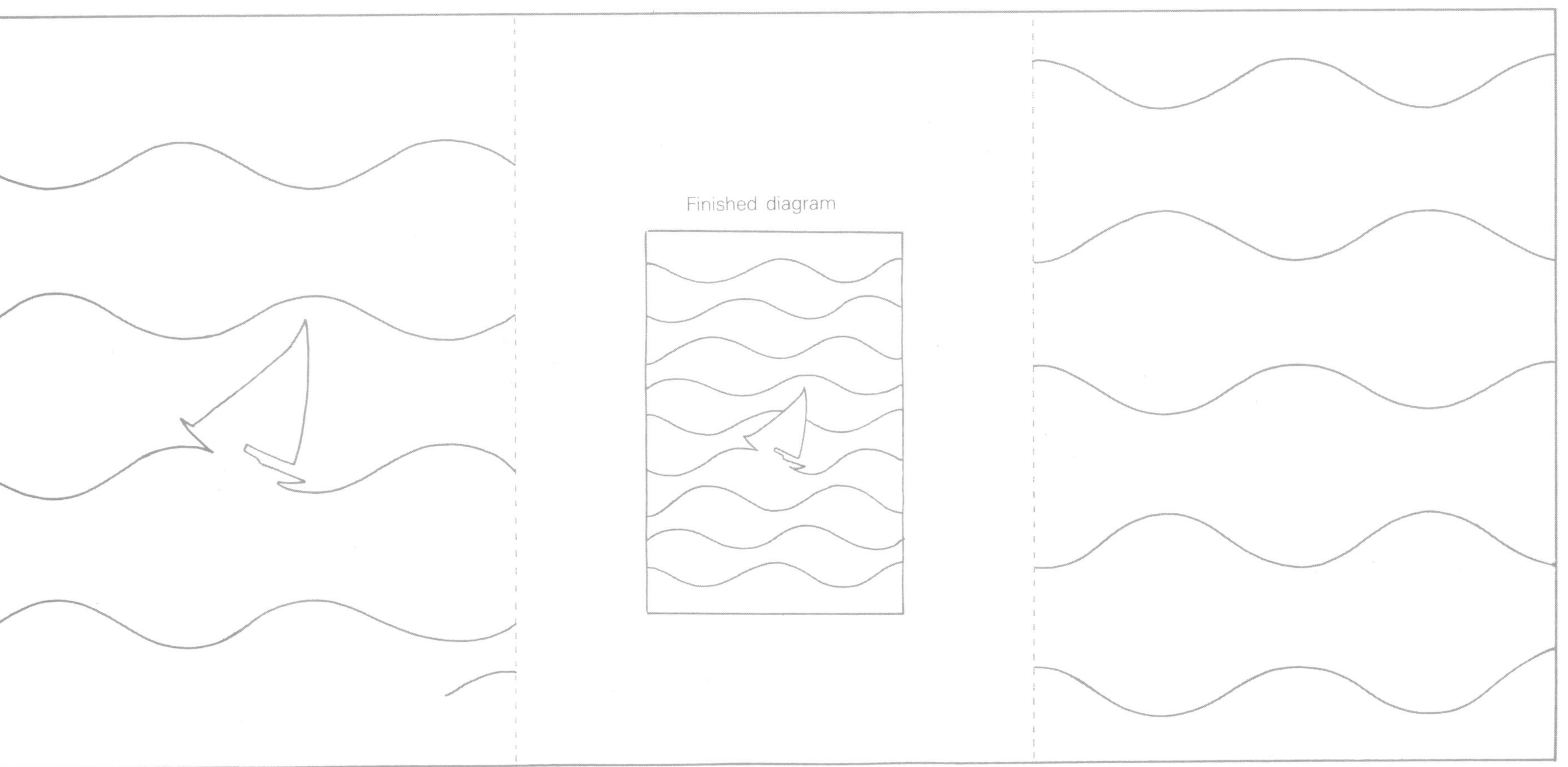